VIOLA VINCENT REPORTING

ANNA KENNA

Tiromoana Publishing

Viola Vincent Reporting

Anna Kenna

Tiromoana Publishing

Print Edition: 978-0-473-38458-6

For more information about this author, visit:
www.annakenna.com and www.facebook.com/abkenna54/

ACKNOWLEDGMENTS

My warmest thanks to Grace Tong for sharing my passion for this story; Sue Reid and her daughters, Rachael and Melissa; Sally Wenley for sharing her world; Paul Norris, Alister Baird and On Yer Bike Paraparaumu, for technical help; and to Vivienne Joseph, for advice and encouragement.

Finally to my family and extended family for their abundant love and support.

FROM THE AUTHOR

'Curiosity killed the cat' is an old saying invented by grown-ups to stop kids asking questions. My dad encouraged me to ask questions and I'm glad he did. I guess that's why I became a journalist. Good journalism is all about asking questions and continuing to ask them even when people don't like it.

Being a bit nosey can be a good thing, especially if your questions result in things changing for the better. Sometimes we accept things in life that don't make sense. For instance, why do we pay for bottled water when it's free from the tap? Why cigarettes are still sold if they kill people, how can we have an obesity epidemic in one part of the world and starvation in another?

A lot of good things have happened by people looking for answers to those sorts of questions. If curiosity killed the cat that's bad news for the cat but unless you have whiskers and a tail, don't be put off. Like Caitlin, the central character of this book, I reckon not being curious enough is a greater risk to the world.

CHAPTER ONE

Finn's death was just the start of what turned out to be the worst day in Caitlin Nove's life. She woke to find his translucent body floating on top of the water like a soggy potato chip. Sobbing, she transported the corpse downstairs and presented it to her mother.

"Poor Finn," said Mum, stepping back and shielding her toast. "Was it the cat?"

"Don't think so," said Caitlin, sniffing loudly. "Probably just old age."

Rita Nove put an arm around her daughter's shoulders. "Well," she said, searching desperately for something comforting to say. "He had . . . a good life . . . didn't he?"

Caitlin pictured Finn swimming alone often in murky water because she hadn't got around to cleaning his bowl. She remembered him being terrorised by Skoota, who'd once batted him right out his bowl onto the carpet. She looked down at Finn's jellied eye staring up at her.

"He had a horrible life," she wailed and ran upstairs.

Caitlin wanted to bury Finn in the garden but her mother said, "Why not flush him down the toilet?"

Caitlin looked horrified. "No way," she said.

"He'll end up back in the sea."

"Goldfish don't come from the sea!"

"Well, the water. You know. Much better than the garden – for a fish."

Caitlin looked doubtful. "What about all the other . . . stuff . . . down there?"

"As long as we flush a couple of times before he goes down, he'll be fine."

"Sure?"

"Sure."

With a look of solemn reverence, Caitlin dropped Finn's tiny body into the toilet bowl and shut her eyes.

Her mother flushed.

Finn's undignified departure from the world, swirling down the U-bend, set Caitlin off on another wave of sobbing. She yanked a length of toilet tissue off the roll and blew her nose.

"Nobody's allowed to use that for the rest of the day," she decreed.

She shooed her mother out of the bathroom and turned on the shower.

After her shower Caitlin rubbed the steamed-up mirror and examined her reflection. Her short hair framed an oval face, still pinkish from the heat. She had her mother's green eyes and her father's jaw, apparently. She had to take her mother's word for that, as she'd never met her father. She moved closer to the mirror and bared her teeth, corralled by a set of braces, just three weeks old. She relaxed her grimace, and mussed her hair into a spiky arrangement with a glob of gel from a jar on the vanity top. She was examining a fresh crop of pimples on her hairline when there was a toot in the driveway.

When Caitlin emerged from the bathroom wrapped in a towel, her mother was at the kitchen sink filling two plastic drink bottles. On the table sat the fruits of her morning's work: a stack of chicken sandwiches wrapped in cling film, a plastic box full of fudge slice, some tumblers and plates, and a bag of kiwifruit.

"Phil's here," said Caitlin, scuttling by. Don't let him use the bathroom, Okay?"

"Right," said Mum, smiling as she lowered the sandwiches into the mouth of a large red backpack.

Caitlin peeked through the blinds and saw Phil standing in the driveway next to his big 4WD. Caitlin thought he looked like one of those male models in a clothing catalogue. He was wearing a dark green fleece jacket, faded jeans and soft tan hiking boots that looked as though they'd only ever scaled escalators and hiked around the shopping mall.

"Hi babe," she heard him say as he swung his arm around her mother's waist. Caitlin shut the blinds with a snap and began raking through her cluttered wardrobe.

THE DRIVE to Redwood Falls took them way beyond the outskirts of the city, through a narrow gorge with a sudsy river rushing far below. The chiselled cliffs dwarfed the truck as it negotiated the twisty road, slowing occasionally to edge past vehicles coming the other way.

"Some awesome tracks out at Redwood," Phil said. He rose in his seat to address Caitlin in the rear-view mirror.

"Yeah?" she said. She flicked her phone buds out of one ear.

"You can ride right over the saddle to the coast."

"Okay."

"But we'll be keeping to the easy tracks today." He nodded pointedly towards the passenger's seat, "for people who're just out of trainer wheels."

Mum punched him on the shoulder and Caitlin forced a smile.

She knew Phil was making an effort but she got a bit tired of guys playing the surrogate dad – and there'd been a few over the years.

Caitlin yawned, stretched and gazed out the window. The road had finally straightened out, the cliffs had given way to gently sloping pastures and the river, its fury spent, flowed placidly between shingle plates.

Phil swung into a parking bay alongside the river.

"Need a pee," he said, "seeing as you wouldn't let me go at your place".

Caitlin and her mum exchanged an amused glance and walked over to the water's edge.

"What a beautiful day," said Mum, peeling off her sweatshirt.

Caitlin watched her copper hair ripple as it settled back on her shoulders. While most of her friend's mums were complaining about going grey and having fortieth birthday parties, Rita Nove was barely thirty.

"What?" asked Mum.

Caitlin quickly looked away. "Nothing. Just looking at the river."

"You girls ready to hit the road?" yelled Phil, crashing out of the bushes and sending a flock of tiny finches into the air.

Caitlin giggled.

"As much grace as a rampaging elephant," Mum whispered.

"Huh?" said Phil. He twanged the ties holding the bikes.

"I said it's nice to be out in the elements." She winked at Caitlin.

Caitlin grinned.

Phil frowned and looked suspiciously from one to the other. "Right. Let's go."

CAITLIN STOOD SQUINTING up at the dense bush. It seemed to hug the hills like a giant beanie. Way up top, a white smudge stood out against the green canopy. From far away the waterfall looked as though it wasn't moving but a distant roar could be heard above the soft chorus of birds.

Phil had parked under the generous shadow of a huge totara. There was only one other vehicle in the car park – a silver station wagon with kayak racks on top.

"Here you go," said Phil, holding Caitlin's bike with one hand as he released her mother's from the T-shaped frame on the back of the vehicle.

"Bit of a clunker, Rita."

He bounced the metallic blue mountain bike onto its tyres.

Mum looked embarrassed.

"That was my Christmas present from Dad."

"Whoops."

Now it was Phil's turn to look embarrassed.

"Sorry. I guess I'm just used to lighter frames."

"And way heavier price tags," said Mum. "You can have your ten-grand, feather-weight super-duper whatever. This is just fine for me."

They pushed their bikes to the start of the track. In the distance the high-pitched whine of trail bikes droned like a persistent mosquito.

"Blasted things shouldn't be allowed in here," said Phil, clicking his helmet strap shut.

Ten minutes later they were riding in single file along a well-worn trail; Caitlin in front, Mum in the middle and Phil coasting behind.

Caitlin came to a fork in the track and started to wobble.

"Which way?" she shouted over her shoulder.

"Left," yelled Phil. "The other way's Devil's Elbow. Not sure you girls are ready for that yet."

Caitlin heard her mum snort.

As they started up a long hill, Phil took the lead.

Caitlin concentrated on the rhythmical pumping of his calf muscles as she puffed along behind.

She glanced over her shoulder at her mum, not far behind.

"So worth it when you get to the top," Phil called over his shoulder, but his words were drowned out by the whine of the trail bikes which seemed to be in the next valley. At the top they stopped to catch their breath.

"Wow," panted Mum, the last to arrive.

"Told you it was worth it," said Phil.

He took a noisy swig from his drink bottle.

They looked down on the treetops, which stretched right across to the coast. Beyond, the sea glinted like exquisite green silk in the morning sun.

Directly below them the bush thinned and the track wound down into a wide valley. Willows lined the banks of the river, dipping their long tendrils into the languid current.

"Lunch at the bottom," said Phil, pushing off. "Take it easy though. It's pretty steep."

Caitlin took a deep breath and followed, a knot of fear and exhilaration bunching her stomach as she gathered speed. The wind whistled past her ears and she locked her elbows against the jittering that set her helmet drumming on her skull.

She was halfway down the slope when something reared into her path. The metallic scream of a motor blasted her eardrums. Hot fumes flooded her nostrils. The wide eyes of the young biker met hers for a fraction of a second as he fought to control his bucking machine. He seemed to stop in midair, feet flailing wildly, before he bounced awkwardly on the other side of the track and accelerated away, spraying gravel and dust.

Caitlin's instinctive swerve sent her careering down a bank. Branches cracked and snapped as the prickly foliage broke her fall. She struggled to her feet and began to stagger up the bank.

"Caitlin!" she heard her mother scream.

It took her a moment to realise the danger wasn't over. For the second time a screaming engine deafened her. She ducked down as another bike soared over her head, rebounded on the other side of the track, and skidded away.

Caitlin got up just in time to see her mother, her feet scudding the ground, her mouth an oval of silent terror as she hurtled down the hill, pedals spinning wildly.

Caitlin's hands sprang to her face. She watched Phil dump his bike and sprint back up the slope. But there was nothing he could do.

The fall, when it came, was surprisingly, deceptively graceful. Her mother's front wheel hit something, a rock or tree root. There was a loud crack as the handlebars snapped off. Caitlin watched as her mother, with a surprised look on her face, somersaulted through the air like some bizarre circus performer, landing with a sickening thud almost on top of the bike.

For a moment there was total silence. Then a couple of tuis began calling to one another. Dust particles drifted downward through shards of golden sunlight.

CHAPTER TWO

Three months later . . .

Caitlin lay on her bed and watched the rain. Wind-driven droplets sprayed like fine gravel against the window. Outside, a plum tree danced loose-limbed in the breeze, occasionally slapping a leafy branch against the windowpane. Caitlin frowned. She'd have to do something about that as soon as the rain stopped. She pictured herself getting the ladder and the long-handled pruners out of the garage – or maybe she'd ask Granddad to do it. She felt guilty. Granddad was doing a lot around the place these days.

There was a soft prow as Skoota jumped onto her bed.

"Hello puss," Caitlin said, jiggling sideways to make room.

The big marmalade cat blinked haughtily then began padding the covers with his white-socked paws.

"Ouch!" yelled Caitlin, as a sharp claw pricked her thigh.

Skoota narrowed his eyes and looked at her for a moment, then plopped down and rested his head on his paws. Lids lowered like shutters over yellow, almond eyes.

Caitlin wriggled her fingers deep into Skoota's warm fur and let her eyes wander around the room. It was hard to think of this as her room now. Although she'd moved in about two months ago, and her things now cluttered surfaces, the essence of her mother still lingered like perfume in the air. There were the vibrant coral and green curtains that Rita had made out of some cheap fabric she found in a sale, the bold painting of a fairground scene she'd struggled home with from the Sunday market, and her favourite antique hat and umbrella stand that now held Caitlin's tatty baseball cap and hockey stick. The big dresser, once displaying her mother's perfumes and face creams, was now a clutter of Caitlin's stuff. There was a disintegrating bird's nest with a broken egg inside, a pack of playing cards, hair gel (lid missing), a tangle of jewellery, pens, pencils, an eraser, coins and a hockey badge with 'most improved player' on it. On top of the jumble was a very dirty, striped sock with a hole in the toe and an empty can of spray deodorant lying on its side.

Caitlin sighed and swung her feet onto the floor.

Downstairs she could hear voices.

She heard the front door close and then the

rubber-tyred squeak of her mother's wheelchair on the polished wooden floor.

Caitlin stood in the kitchen doorway watching her mother trying to manoeuvre into the pantry. She was going backwards and forwards trying to reach a box of cereal on a shelf just above her head.

Caitlin held back, her hands by her sides, fingers twitching. She was close enough to see her mother's neck muscles tense and hear the grunt as she leaned forward grasping at the cereal box. Her fingertips brushed the packet but couldn't get a grip. Caitlin looked away. There was a soft thud as the box hit the floor, discharging a cascade of yellow flakes.

"I'll get it," said Caitlin in a thin cheery voice.

She saw her mother's shoulders stiffen, her fists clench. She swore, pushed herself backwards then spun around and freewheeled into the dining room.

Skoota, who'd just sauntered into the kitchen looking for his breakfast, skidded out of the way and, with a startled backward glance, flung himself through the cat door.

Caitlin picked up the cereal box and cleaned up the spillage.

She glanced over at her mother sitting near the window and reached for the hot water jug.

"Coffee?" she asked, easing the lid off a plastic container.

There was no reply.

"Mum?"

Nothing. She made the coffee anyway.

A few months ago, she wouldn't have known where to start, but now she put four generous spoons of coffee into the plunger, carefully poured in the boiling water and set it aside to brew.

She turned on the radio.

"It's the weekend!" a DJ boomed in a deep male voice. *"Skies clearing later folks, so no excuse to stay inside and blob out. There's the Valley outdoor music concert, the Pinehill Forest 10k fun run and . . ."*

Caitlin switched it off, poured the coffee and took it over to her mother.

"Thanks," she said with a taut smile.

She wrapped her freshly-polished fingernails around the mug.

"Cool," said Caitlin, inspecting her mother's hand. "Sonya do that?"

"Yep."

Sonya came daily to help while her mother adjusted to life in a wheelchair.

"Nice colour," said Caitlin brightly.

"Mmmm," said her mother, taking a sip of coffee.

Caitlin fixed herself some cereal and sat down at the breakfast bar.

Her mother, smartly dressed, as always, in a lemon T-shirt and navy track pants, continued to stare past the rain-smeared glass to a place where

Caitlin couldn't reach her. It'd been like this for the two weeks since she'd been home from the spinal unit. The doctors had said it could take months for her to come to terms with being paraplegic, but nothing could prepare Caitlin for those days when Rita seemed to fizz with irritation, as brittle as ice on a winter puddle. Other times there'd be tears, fumbly hugs, unfinished sentences and long silences that made Caitlin's chest ache.

She was spooning the last of the cereal into her mouth when the phone rang.

"Hi Granddad," she said, brushing her hand up and down the bristly hair at the base of her neck.

"Hi, precious. How is she?"

Caitlin glanced over at her mother, still sitting at the window, slowly twirling her coffee cup between her elegant fingers.

"You know."

"One of those days?"

"Yup," she said.

"Mmmm," said Granddad. "I'm on my way. Just got to pick up some stuff at the hardware store."

CHAPTER THREE

The stiff bristles of the new paintbrush drew a slick of white enamel along the window frame. Caitlin, the tip of her tongue clamped firmly between her teeth, finished the action with an exaggerated flick of the wrist.

She stepped back and collided with Granddad, who was working on the opposite wall.

"Oi," he said straightening up and grimacing as he flexed his back.

"Still think aubergine would have been better," Caitlin said, screwing up her face.

"Nah, white's best for a bathroom. Fresher, more . . ."

"Boring," said Caitlin.

The new wheelchair-sized bathroom had been added to Caitlin's old room downstairs. It had been built pretty quickly while her mum was in the spinal unit but Granddad got sick of waiting for the tradesmen to paint it so he decided to do it himself.

He bent down, stuck the lid back on the paint tin and tapped the rim with the butt of a screwdriver. "Right," he said, with a weary sigh. "While that's drying, let's deal to that tree."

Out in the yard, Caitlin held the ladder as Granddad lopped some branches off the plum tree. As he climbed down he paused and snapped the pruning shears at Mum who was watching them through the window. The metal blades clicked like a sharp beak and Granddad squawked, like a parrot.

Caitlin watched her mum force a smile and open the window. "Some food here when you're ready," she said.

"Wark, wark. We'll be right there," said Granddad, snapping the blades in time with his voice.

"That's good," he whispered to Caitlin, as the window closed.

"Yeah," said Caitlin, "she is trying."

"Phil been in touch?"

"Yesterday. He said he'd take her out somewhere over the weekend."

"She going?"

"What do you think?"

"Pity."

After they'd had some food Granddad took the pruning shears to other parts of the garden, while Caitlin grabbed the broom from outside the back door and swept the drive. She was going to put it back on the porch but Granddad suggested she put it in the garage, out of the way.

Caitlin heaved on the heavy roller door, stiff from lack of use. As it slid open a musty smell engulfed her and she sneezed. She pushed the door fully up and daylight rolled over a blue station wagon, parked slightly crookedly, its front bumper touching the back wall. That's the only way it would fit in the garage.

She sighed as she remembered how her mother would stretch over the steering wheel, neck forward, peering over the bonnet as she edged the car forward until the bumper gently nudged the garage wall. It seemed a lifetime ago. She swallowed and peered inside the car. On the back seat was a folded picnic rug; pine needles stuck into the tight weave like tiny spears. Beside it were a kebab wrapper, a half empty water bottle and a pamphlet on Marshall's Crossing – the walk she and her mother had done the week before Christmas.

Caitlin opened the door to retrieve them and something else caught her eye. Lying on the floor behind the driver's seat were her mother's hiking boots.

Caitlin picked them up and began to dislodge crusts of dry mud with her fingernail. A stale earthy smell tickled her nostrils and took her back to the bush, memories of mossy trails, sun-dappled tracks and her mother's mud-flecked calf muscles leading the way.

She sighed heavily, gently tucked the laces inside

the boots and pushed them behind some big paint tins on a high shelf. Wrestling the garage door closed, Caitlin heard a car in the driveway and turned to see a police 4WD pulling up. She watched her granddad wipe his hands on his overalls and usher a young policeman into the house. Not wanting to miss anything, Caitlin hurried after them.

The policeman looked apologetic as he started to explain why he'd come. Caitlin heard the words "nothing illegal" and "no grounds to prosecute". She looked at Granddad who reached out and drew her near.

"So those little beggars are going to get away with it," he said loudly, a look of disgust on his face.

The policeman looked towards the front door as though anxious to escape, and turned his hat over in his hands.

"I'm sorry," he said, "but the bikers weren't actually on the track – which would have been unlawful – they just crossed it."

Caitlin watched her granddad shake his head. "They were hooning about," he said, his Adam's apple bobbing the words out, "with no thought for public safety."

The policeman looked at the floor again. "They might not be your cup of tea, sir, nor mine, but the kids were doing what trail bikers do - zooming around the countryside."

"And knocking innocent people down," said Granddad. There was an awkward silence.

Caitlin's mum cleared her throat. "Well, thanks for com—"

But Granddad hadn't finished. "And it's taken you three months to tell us this," he said.

The policeman shrugged. "It was fully investigated, sir, I assure you."

"Ha!" said Granddad. He released Caitlin and rose from the table, ushering the constable to the door.

Before he left, the policeman went around to the back of his vehicle and hauled out a long package. It was wrapped in black plastic and tied with string. "I'm obliged to return this to you," he said, grimly, lying what looked like a bony corpse on the ground. He closed the tailgate and turned to Granddad. "As I said, we couldn't find anything criminal . . ." He hesitated and nudged the package with his boot. "But you might want to look into why that bike snapped the way it did."

Caitlin stared at the ungainly bundle lying at their feet. Images flashed through her mind. Pedals spinning wildly, the front wheel hitting something and the slow-motion replay of her mother tumbling through the air, still holding imaginary handlebars, as though she could steer herself to safety. A strange weakness travelled though her body, the sound of helicopter blades thumped in her head . . . and moaning . . . the sound of her mother moaning as they eased the stretcher into the belly of the chopper.

A toot from the departing police vehicle interrupted Caitlin's thoughts. She shuddered.

Granddad was stooping to pick up the bike, a look of distaste on his face as though he'd been asked to dispose of a maggoty cat. He turned to Caitlin. "Help your mother inside," he said gruffly. "I'll take care of this."

CHAPTER FOUR

Caitlin kept chewing over what the policeman had said as though it was a stale piece of gum she just couldn't spit out. She was mulling it over in Social Studies the next day when Mrs Bowman pounced.

"Caitlin, could you please repeat my home-work instructions?" Caitlin felt her cheeks burn. Above her oblong glasses Mrs Bowman's pencilled eyebrows arched with expectation. "Well?"

"Ah, um . . ." Caitlin looked down at her desktop.

Mrs Bowman sighed and turned to a dark girl beside her. "Ella, perhaps you could brief Caitlin after class."

Ella Peebles nodded smugly as the bell rang for the break. Caitlin didn't give Ella the satisfaction of passing on the homework. Instead she huddled with Brooke and Olivia and copied the instructions into her book.

Research a person who lived in the 1950s. Find out as much as you can about their life. This person could be a relative or a friend. Ask your parents and grandparents. Search out family photos. Due April 30.

"How's your Mum?" Brooke asked, stuffing her book back into her school bag and pulling out an apple.

"Fine," said Caitlin delving into her lunchbox. "Her work's given her some stuff to do at home."

"That's good," said Olivia, smiling. "Eh?"

"Yeah." Caitlin wasn't so sure. Sitting at a desk had never been her mum's thing. She worked as an occupational therapist at Pinehaven Retirement Village. It was like a sick joke really. Here she was, stuck in a wheelchair, being paid to help keep people active.

Olivia caught the look on Caitlin's face and quickly turned to Brooke. "Who're you going to do your project on?"

Brooke screwed up her face. "Pass".

"Caitlin?"

"Dunno either. I think everybody in our family's totally boring."

~

"YOUR GREAT AUNT VIOLA. That's who you should do it on," said Granddad as they drove home from hockey practice. "She'd make a fascinating study."

"Hmm," said Caitlin, twiddling the car radio till she found Grunt FM.

Granddad frowned. "You're named after her."

"Who?"

"Turn it down! Your Aunt Viola."

"Don't remind me." Caitlin pulled a face. "Caitlin Viola. Fancy being named after an overgrown violin."

Granddad shook his head and sighed. "A flower also, actually. Anyway, she was an amazing woman, Viola. A journalist."

Caitlin yawned. "What's for tea?"

"Pizza," said Granddad. "Homemade."

"Cool."

When they got home Caitlin's mum was working on the computer, converting the retirement village's old records into computer files.

"Riveting stuff," she said rolling her eyes and turning the computer off.

"Caitlin needs to know about Viola," said Granddad quickly changing the subject.

"Viola. Why?"

"School project," said Caitlin, screwing up her face.

"Okay," said Mum, looking thoughtful. "You're named . . ."

"I know," groaned Caitlin.

"Actually, the research has already been done," said Granddad.

"Huh?" said Caitlin.

Her mother sighed, as if it was all too much effort. "Your grandma always talked about writing a book about Viola. She was in the middle of researching it when . . ." Caitlin noticed Granddad shift uncomfortably. "Anyway, she got hold of heaps of stuff. It's all here somewhere. I'll look later."

"Okay," shrugged Caitlin, "but what was so special about Aunt Viola?"

Caitlin's mother looked reflective. "She was a pretty amazing woman."

"Amazing . . . in what way?"

"Gutsy."

"What do you mean?"

"Unconventional, I suppose you'd say."

"A little crazy." Granddad chuckled.

"No that's not fair," said Rita.

Caitlin rolled her eyes. Lately it seemed her mother had lost her sense of humour as well as the use of her legs.

"She was determined – feisty –" she said, "in the days when women were supposed to be quiet and demure."

"Give me a quiet, demure woman any day," joked Granddad, heading for the kitchen.

"Was she very famous?" Caitlin asked her mother.

"She was. She worked on some big stories. Upset a lot of people."

"Yeah?" Caitlin was beginning to like the sound of Great Aunt Viola.

Caitlin joined Granddad in the kitchen and began spooning cat food into a chunky china bowl with black paw prints over it. Skoota paced the floor, fluffy tail erect, purring with ecstasy, as the smell of Gourmet Ocean Selection tormented his twitchy nostrils. Caitlin decided to raise the subject that had been knocking on the inside of her skull like a woodpecker for most of the day. "Granddad," she asked, "What did that policeman mean the other day?"

"How?" Granddad was distracted, peering into the fridge. "Olives!" he yelled. "Rita, where did you say they were?"

"Top shelf, at the back," Caitlin's mum called from the lounge. "Should be, anyway."

Granddad poked his head further into the fridge. "Ah. Got 'em." He turned to Caitlin. "Sorry, pet. What were you saying?"

"The policeman, the other day," said Caitlin, delivering dinner to Skoota, who practically climbed into the bowl before it hit the floor. "What he said about the bike."

"Huh?"

Caitlin frowned. "You know. He said something about looking into something to do with the bike."

Granddad was slicing olives with a small knife and sprinkling them on the pizzas. "What for?" he said. "If those damn kids hadn't been skylarking around, your mother wouldn't have ended up" – he lowered his voice and nodded in the direction of the lounge – "like that."

"But the handlebars shouldn't have broken off, should they?"

"Pass me the oregano love." Caitlin reached into the pantry.

"Here. Granddad?"

"What?"

"The handlebars. How come they snapped off?"

"Blast!" Granddad's heavy hands upended the box of herbs. "That was clumsy."

"Here." Caitlin picked up the pizza and began blowing the excess oregano off into the sink.

"No, Caitlin!" Granddad yelled. "That's unhygienic."

He shook his head and pretended to cuff her around the ear. "Monster. Now set the table. There's a good girl. These will be ready in about ten minutes." Granddad slid the pizzas into the oven and closed the door.

Caitlin sighed and went off to get the tablemats.

CHAPTER FIVE

Just as Caitlin was starting on her fifth slice of pizza, a vehicle pulled up the driveway.

"It's Phil," she reported, peering through the kitchen window. She noticed her mother stiffen.

Granddad looked pleased and tense at the same time. "Good to see you," he said, as Phil eased his lanky frame through the door. "You eaten? Plenty here . . . can I get you a beer?"

"No, nothing thanks," said Phil, holding his huge paddle of a palm up like a policeman stopping traffic. "I'm just on my way to the gym. Thought I'd call in and . . . Hi Rita." He walked around to the other side of the table and stooped awkwardly to kiss Caitlin's mum on the cheek.

Her smile was fleeting. As Phil straightened up his head bonged a low-slung light. Its beam swept across the table like a frantic searchlight until

Granddad reached up and steadied it. Everybody laughed. For a moment it was like old times.

Caitlin kept giggling long after everyone had stopped. Her mother frowned across the table and she tried to stop but ended up snorting, which earned her an even sterner look.

"So, how's it going?" asked Phil, smiling at Caitlin and rubbing his head. The question hung in the air like a swollen rain cloud.

"Can't complain," said Granddad. He glanced apologetically at Caitlin's mother. "We get by."

There was another awkward silence. Phil jumped in. "Hey, Rita, I was talking to this guy at the gym. He said he can work out a fitness programme for you. Weights and stuff." Caitlin watched a veil fall across her mother's features.

"Yeah?" she said, studying the tablecloth.

"Yeah," said Phil, not seeming to notice the warning signs. "For upper-body strength. They have lots of people in wheel– I mean, like you, going there," he finished lamely.

Caitlin felt the air freeze. She watched her mother flick her hair back over her shoulder. Her eyes slid away from Phil's enthusiastic gaze. Caitlin thought he looked like a puppy that had just dropped a stick nobody wanted to play with.

"Great," said Granddad.

"Yeah," continued Phil, glad of some support. "Be good for you."

Caitlin watched her mother strike like a cornered

snake. "I think I can decide what's good for me," she said, her eyes flashing.

Caitlin looked away. Her foot assumed a life of its own, jiggling under the table. She dug her fingernails into her palm. Granddad fussed like a broody hen, offering everybody coffee and talking flat out. A short time later, when Phil got up to go, Caitlin followed him out to the driveway.

"Thanks for coming," she said in a quiet voice

"No problem." Phil shrugged and looked down the street. Caitlin felt sorry for him. It wasn't just tonight. Even at the hospital Caitlin noticed the way her mother seemed to look past him and react irritably to almost everything he said. Caitlin didn't know why he kept coming but she admired him for it.

"Sorry," she said. "She just gets . . ."

Phil waved his hand. "It's okay. I shouldn't have pushed it." His face softened. "How are you doing?"

Caitlin blushed. "Good," she said quickly. She pushed her finger through a layer of yellow dust coating Phil's normally sparkling vehicle.

"Been doing a bit of work in the forestry block," he said, reading her thoughts.

CLEAN ME! Caitlin wrote in big letters. Phil laughed. There was a long silence and then Caitlin said, "The policeman said there might've been something wrong with the bike."

Phil rubbed his chin and squinted into the distance. "Doesn't surprise me," he said. "I've thought that myself."

"Why didn't you—"

"Mention it? Well . . . didn't seem much point. What's happened . . ."

"But people shouldn't sell bikes that aren't safe."

"'Course, but . . ."

"The handlebars snapped."

"Yeah, but maybe she would have got hurt just as badly anyway."

"Maybe she wouldn't."

Phil sighed and began tracing a pattern of his own on the dusty bodywork. Suddenly he looked intently at Caitlin. "I reckon leave it, eh?"

"But—"

"Dragging the whole thing up will only upset your mother."

"Like, she's not upset already!" Caitlin didn't mean to raise her voice. She looked down and squeezed her eyes tight.

Phil reached out and patted her shoulder. "I'm sorry," he said. "I wish I could turn the clock back . . . every day."

Caitlin looked up. "You?"

"If I hadn't taken you there . . ."

"Wasn't your fault," she said, "and Mum doesn't think that. No way."

Phil shrugged. "I'm not so sure." He kicked a loose paving stone jutting above the others. "Anyway, gotta go," he said, opening the vehicle door and easing himself behind the wheel. He started the engine, shifted the gear lever and then poked his head out the window. He hesitated for a moment and then said, "See if you can find a receipt for that bike – or some guarantee – that'd be the place to start."

CAITLIN HAULED her track pants out of a tangle of dirty laundry in the washing machine. She sniffed them to make sure they weren't too gross and then flung them into the hallway, where she knew she wouldn't miss them next morning. She sprinkled soap powder onto the rest of the load and turned the washing machine on. Since Granddad had left that evening she'd been avoiding her mother and, as much as she hated chores, they were providing a welcome distraction.

She was in the kitchen making her school lunch when she heard the TV turned off. Moments later her mother rolled in behind her. "I'll do that," she said, wheeling herself towards the bench.

Caitlin slapped down two slices of frozen bread. "It's fine," she said, without looking around. Walking briskly past her mother, she opened the refrigerator and reached for the butter

"I'll do it," her mother tried again, reaching out. Caitlin ignored her and began smearing butter in brisk careless strokes, covering the bench as well as the bread.

There was a long silence then her mother said, "I know I'm pretty useless but I'm sure I can—"

Caitlin whirled around. "Stop saying stuff like that." The words whistled across the top of her mother's head.

"What?" asked her mother, looking stunned.

"About being useless."

"It was a joke."

"Yeah. Right." Caitlin scowled.

Her mother looked hurt. "What's wrong?"

"Nothing wrong with me," snapped Caitlin, ripping the bread with a stab of the knife.

"Caitlin."

"I'm not the one being mean to everyone."

Caitlin let go of the knife and it clattered to the floor, flicking greasy yellow specks over the lower cupboard doors. She marched out of the kitchen and up the stairs to her room. She went to slam the door but a mud-caked trainer got in the way. Instead of the house-rattling bang she intended, there was a pathetic rubber thud.

CHAPTER SIX

Caitlin's eyelids fluttered like lazy butterflies as the sunlight shone through her bedroom window. She'd forgotten to shut the curtains the night before and a soft radiant light flooded her room. Yanking the covers up, Caitlin rolled over, aware of a dull ache in her belly. She stretched out her legs to try and ease it, and dozed off again.

When she opened her eyes, she was looking at a photo on her bedside table. She and her mother looked out from the glass frame, their heads pressed together in a picture of cosy happiness

The photo had been taken by her mum's friend, Nina, at the school fair last summer. Just out of frame, Caitlin remembered, she was clutching a rag doll with outrageous orange hair that she'd won in a quick-fire raffle and which was now slumped on a wicker chair in the corner of her room. It must have been the last photo she'd had taken before she got braces. Her teeth were as unrestrained as her smile. Chin jutting forward, she was beaming into the lens. Her mother was laughing at some shared joke.

Caitlin pulled the covers up over her head and tried to shut out memories of her behaviour the night before. In the warm darkness her watch beeped. She illuminated the dial. Eight o'clock! Why hadn't her mother called her? With a fresh flush of guilt she remembered she'd turned the intercom off. She flicked it on and heard the faint hum of her mother and Sonya talking downstairs.

"Morning," she said.

"There you are," said her mother, sounding relieved. "I was going to send Sonya up to see where you'd got to."

"Just having a shower."

"Okay

In a flurry of cast-off covers Caitlin scampered out of bed and across the hallway to the bathroom. Moments later she was gaping in horror at strawberry-red stains on her pyjama pants.

Back in her room, her hand hovered over the intercom button for a moment and then she realised Sonya would hear everything and she changed her mind. She rummaged in her school bag for the sanitary pad that had been given out by the school nurse after a lesson on periods last term. As she ripped it out of the cheerful packaging, Caitlin was glad she hadn't stuck it on the back of an unknowing male classmate, like most of the other girls had. She went back to the bathroom, stuffed her soiled pyjamas into the laundry hamper and jumped in the shower.

After a doubtful glance out the window Caitlin grabbed her new singlet top and pulled it on. She, Brooke and Olivia had each bought one in a different colour at an end of summer sale and had made a pact to wear them to school on Monday. She looked in the mirror and frowned. Goosebumps had already sprouted on her arms.

Caitlin sprinted downstairs and into the kitchen to get her school lunch. She kicked the butter knife, still lying where it had bounced off the bench the night before. She bit her lip as she picked it up and slid it into the cutlery basket of the dishwasher. On the bench her lunch sat neatly stacked. A pack of sandwiches, a box of raisins, a green apple and some new rice snacks her mother thought were healthier than potato chips. Caitlin slipped them into her bag and headed down the hallway to her mother's bedroom.

Sonya was making the bed, her dreadlocks bouncing as she tucked in the sheets. "Hi," she said, as Caitlin hovered.

She still found it hard to have a relative stranger sharing the house so early in the morning. "Hi," she said and smiled. She went over to the bathroom and knocked on the half open door. "Mum?"

"Hi sweetheart," said her mother, pulling the door open. Caitlin's bare feet registered the cold tiles in the spacious bathroom that still smelled of new paint. Her mother, dressed in a pale blue robe, was sitting in her wheelchair about to get into the shower. Her hair was pulled into an untidy topknot, loose strands falling across her thin face. A wave of pity caught Caitlin off guard and her eyes welled.

"Hey," said her mother holding her arms out. Caitlin stumbled forward and buried her head in her mother's warm shoulder. "Sorry," she mumbled.

"So am I," Mum whispered into Caitlin's hair, "for being such a grump." Caitlin began to sob. "Sonya?" called her mother, after moment or two. "I'd love a coffee."

"Huh?" said Sonya, peering around the door. "You've just had . . . oh, right." She quickly backed out. "One coffee coming up."

Caitlin waited until she heard Sonya clattering about in the kitchen, then she said in a quivery voice. "I've got my period."

"Oh, sweetheart," said her mother, giving her a squeeze. Something crashed in the kitchen.

"Oh crap!" yelled Sonya, then "Whoops, sorry!"

Rita shook her head and Caitlin couldn't help laughing in spite of her tears. She straightened up and wiped her eyes. Her mother reached out and gently tilted her daughter's chin. "You okay?"

"Yep," sniffed Caitlin. "I had a . . . thing . . . pad . . . in my bag."

"You'll need some more." Rita opened the vanity unit and gestured towards a blue package at the back of the cupboard. "Pop some in your bag." Caitlin pulled out the package and took out several pads. She looked around furtively before stuffing them under her top.

Her mother smiled. "No cramps, pains?"

"Little bit."

"If it gets bad, come home, okay?"

"Mmmm."

"Seriously."

"Ye-e-ss!" Caitlin frowned.

Her mum reached out and mussed her hair. "My baby's growing up," she said, a soppy look on her face.

"Mum!" Caitlin protested.

"Well . . ."

"Brooke and Olivia haven't got theirs yet."

"Ah ha."

Caitlin pouted. "It's not fair."

"I started at twelve," said her mother.

"Mmmm."

"You usually follow your mother."

"Gee, thanks Mum."

Rita laughed then frowned at her daughter's bare arms. "You going to be warm enough?"

"Yep."

"Sure?"

"I'm fine

"Okay," said her mother, unconvinced. "Make sure you've got a sweatshirt."

Sonya appeared with the coffee and Caitlin scurried off to finish getting ready for school. When she got back, her mother was in the shower and steam was billowing out of the bathroom.

"Bye!" Caitlin called.

"Bye, love!" yelled her mother. "Did you get some breakfast?"

"Yep." It was partly true. Caitlin had a banana in her pocket, which she might get a chance to eat before class.

She had her hand on the front door handle when her mother called again. Caitlin hurried back and had to go into the bathroom to hear her over the roar of the shower. Her mother's pink face popped out from behind the curtain. "Remember I've got an appointment at the unit this afternoon, so you're going to Granddad's."

"Yeah," said Caitlin, jiggling.

"Oh, and . . ."

"Mum, I'm really late!"

"Yeah, sorry. I found some stuff on Viola last night. It's on the hall table."

"Cool," said Caitlin. "Thanks." She grabbed a big brown envelope from beside the phone, stuffed it in her school bag and sprinted out the door.

CHAPTER SEVEN

By the time Caitlin coasted through the school gates on her bike, the bell had already rung. "Get off and walk. You know better than that," said Mr Gifkins, who seemed to appear from nowhere. Caitlin got off her bike, ran up the driveway and locked it into the rack. The first thing she noticed, when she walked into her classroom, was that Brooke and Olivia weren't wearing their singlet tops.

"Aw, you promised," Caitlin said, frowning. "I said if it was nice," said Olivia, gnawing a fingernail.

"Mum wouldn't let me," babbled Brooke, her eyes darting away from Caitlin's reproachful glance. Caitlin scowled and shivered.

"It looks cool though," enthused Olivia, nodding at Caitlin's top.

"You should have rung and told me you'd chickened out," Caitlin said.

She began to tremble, with cold and humiliation. She noticed Ella Peebles, snug in a soft pink polar fleece, sniggering with her friends in the corner.

Mrs Bowman swept into the room and called the class to order. "First things first," she said. "We need some nominations for the school council."

Ella flicked her dark ponytail and looked at her friends expectantly. One of them quickly nominated her and her name was put on the whiteboard. Craig Watters, whose father was a district councillor, was also nominated – to nobody's surprise. As Mrs Bowman scanned the classroom, Brooke, anxious to make amends, called out Caitlin's name. Caitlin glowered at her friend. "I don't want to!" she hissed. But it was too late. Her name joined the others on the board.

"Right," said Mrs Bowman, stabbing a full stop. "We're doing things a little differently this year." To groans from the nominees she outlined how they each had to find something they felt could be improved around the school and give a speech about it. "The successful candidate will be the one who gets the most votes for his or her speech."

"Thanks a bunch," growled Caitlin at morning break. Brooke handed her a chocolate frog and didn't ask for anything in return.

After break the class was given time to work on their 1950s profiles in the library. Caitlin sighed and hauled out the brown envelope. Inside were some newspaper clippings and two photos. She picked up the first and studied the image of a slim young woman in a heavy, double-breasted coat. She was standing by a flowering bush, her gloved hands clasped in front of her and a serious look on her face. There was something familiar in the tilt of her head and the eyes that seemed to draw Caitlin into the grainy detail of the photo.

"Who's that?" asked Olivia.

"My great aunt Viola."

"VI–O–LA!" Olivia spluttered. "You're kidding me!"

Caitlin frowned.

Olivia flushed and looked back at the photo. "She looks like you."

"Yeah?"

"Yeah. 'Cept for the hair."

"That's what mine would be like if I grew it."

"You so should."

Mrs Bowman looked over and frowned. As Olivia turned back to her work, Caitlin picked up the second photo. This one had been taken in a studio. The woman in this photo was older and broader but with the same defiant eyes and wild hair. She was dressed in a high-collared white blouse and tweed jacket. Again her head was tilted, but this time her features were softened by a shy smile. Caitlin smiled back and immediately felt silly. She looked around to make sure no one had seen, slid the photos back into the envelope and took out the clippings. She carefully unfolded the first and squinted at the faded print. The headline read:

Baby Deaths Linked to Colic Remedy
By Viola Saunders
The deaths of three babies in the county in June are being linked to a popular colic remedy, Dewars' Tummy Tamer. Health authorities have removed all stocks of Dewars' from the shelves and have issued notices warning parents not to use the product until further notice.

A handwritten note in the margin said *County Courier, May 5th 1952*. Caitlin carefully unfolded another clipping and read:

'Filthy' Factory Blamed for Killer Baby Tonic
By Viola Saunders
A judge today described conditions in a factory producing baby products as 'utterly filthy'. Justice Thomas Wakeham was presiding over the prosecution of two company directors charged with criminal negligence over the deaths of thirteen infants.

The babies, ranging between newborn and

eighteen months, died after being given Dewars' Tummy Tamer Colic remedy.

The judge praised the work of the County Courier *in uncovering the extent of the contamination and alerting appropriate authorities.*

With a start, Caitlin became aware her classmates were packing up around her. Olivia and Brooke were already standing by the door, gesturing impatiently. Caitlin took her time folding the fragile papers and carefully sliding them back into the envelope, along with the photos.

After lunch, while her friends were shooting hoops, Caitlin tucked a sanitary pad up her sleeve and headed for the girls' toilets. She usually managed to get through the school day without having to use the toilet and the stench that hit her before she'd even pushed open the door reminded her why. She checked the first cubicle to find there was no toilet paper. In the second, the toilet was blocked. The third had both a functioning toilet and toilet paper, but the floor was sodden. Caitlin was glad of her thick-soled shoes.

Caitlin left the cubicle and went to wash her hands in the scum-coated metal basin. There was no soap and the roller-towel dispenser was broken – and looked as if it had been for months. Caitlin shrugged irritably. She wondered if she had PMS. Life suddenly seemed so much more complicated.

CHAPTER EIGHT

"How was your day?" enquired Granddad as they headed home, Caitlin's bike in the back of his little hatchback.

"Great," said Caitlin, pulling a sulky face. "I got nominated for the school council."

Granddad's tufted eyebrows shot upwards. "Did you now? That's fantastic."

"Not."

Granddad looked over at Caitlin, slumped in the passenger's seat like a limp celery stalk. He chuckled. "I think we need some food, fast."

Caitlin perked up. "Fast food?"

"Nice try," said Granddad as he merged into the traffic. "No . . . I have something much better."

The aroma of freshly baked scones greeted Caitlin as she slid open the door to Granddad's little flat. "Yum," she said, ditching her school bag and heading for the kitchen.

"Excuse me?" said Granddad, hands on hips, nodding at her bag.

"Whoops, sorry." Caitlin scooped up the bag and dumped it in the laundry.

"And wash your hands."

Caitlin rolled a slippery bar of manly-smelling soap around in her hands, and dried them on a threadbare tartan towel hanging on a hook beside the basin. On the windowsill stood a green ceramic mug with a solitary toothbrush, one of those double-bristled ones for cleaning dentures. Next to it was a matching stick deodorant and aftershave, part of a father's day gift Rita had given him.

Caitlin always tried to avoid looking at herself in Granddad's magnifying shaving mirror. It made her skin look like orange peel and her pimples, like small volcanoes. She grabbed the hand towel again and wiped down the hand basin. Granddad's tidiness, a legacy of his days in the army, was infectious. Caitlin remembered how reluctant he'd been to move out of the big house after Grandma died and it had taken Rita a lot of talking to persuade him to. But from the moment the real estate agent showed them the little brick unit, he had a miraculous change of mind. "This'll do me," he'd said, and moved in the following week.

The unit was on the end of a row of three, each with a garage and its own little garden, which Granddad had turned into a cheerful display of flowers. There were ruby red camellias, delicate climbing roses hugging a wooden arch and ponga logs bordering raised flowerbeds that became an explosion of colour in the spring. In the corner of the section, bordered by wooden planks, was a vegetable plot with feathery carrot and parsnip stalks just starting to show and a plastic hothouse with lettuces and cherry tomatoes hanging like giant Jaffas from the staked-up vines.

As Granddad buttered the scones, Caitlin hauled herself onto a stool and began to chatter. "You know Kirsty Davies, our hockey captain?" she said. "She broke her finger at practice the other day."

"That right?" said Granddad spreading a slick of raspberry jam over a layer of butter.

Caitlin stared out the window and scowled. "I so don't want to be on the school council. I've got to do this dumb speech."

"You'll be great."

"Hmm."

Granddad pushed the plate of scones towards Caitlin, who grabbed one and demolished most of it in one bite.

"Granddad," she said, chewing thoughtfully, "do you think Mum will get that car? You know, with the hand controls?"

Granddad sighed and looked up. "Who knows, pet? I hope so. Isn't that what she's got the meeting about today?"

"Don't know," said Caitlin. "Maybe. Can I have another scone?"

"Yes," frowned Granddad, "but it's may. May I have another scone? And a 'please' wouldn't go astray either. Yes you may. As long as you butter me one too."

While Caitlin busied herself getting more scones, Granddad began cleaning Buddie's cage. Buddie was Granddad's budgie, a rather odd little bird with sticky-out feathers and a head that looked too big for his body. Caitlin wondered how such an ugly bird could be so obsessed with looking at himself in the mirror.

She put two scones on the breakfast bar and sucked her fingers noisily, earning a disapproving look from Granddad. She pulled a cheeky face and eased herself back onto the barstool. As she watched Granddad fill a small plastic water dish and click it into place between the bars of Buddie's cage, she wondered what she and her mum would have done without him over the last few months. He – and Buddie, much to Skoota's delight – had moved in while her mother was recovering from the accident. He'd cooked, cleaned, and taken Caitlin everywhere she needed to go, including the spinal unit, which was two hours drive away, every weekend. He'd even made some of his famous scones for the school fête and helped on the smash-a-plate stall for the whole afternoon. Caitlin envied his easy way of dealing with her mother. When she was tearful and angry he seemed to know just what to say and, when there was nothing to say, he knew how to listen. But Caitlin sometimes saw the sadness too; how it dulled his eyes and etched deeper lines in his weathered face.

She watched him remove Buddie's seed dish and take it over to the sliding door. A sudden gust ruffled his wavy grey hair as he gently shook the dish just outside the door. An obliging breeze whisked away a cloud of golden flakes. "All husk," said Granddad nodding at Buddie. "Poor little fella. No wonder you're hungry."

Buddie shuffled along the perch and squawked loudly. Tut-tutting and sounding curiously like Buddie himself, Granddad went to the pantry and began shifting stuff about, peering behind tall cereal boxes, and stooping stiffly to scan the lower shelves. "Damn," he said finally. "Right out of Buddie tucker. I'll have to go to the shops."

Caitlin decided to stay and do her homework but gave Granddad a list of a few things they needed at home.

"Where do I find these?" he said, pointing at 'sanitary pads - with wings'.

"Near the soap and shampoo and stuff," said Caitlin blushing.

"Your mum usually gets Sonya to get her supplies."

"They're for me," Caitlin mumbled.

"Right," said Granddad, dropping the car keys and fumbling around on the floor to retrieve them. He straightened up. "Right. Right then, I'll be off."

He scurried out the door then came back. "Oh, while I remember, I've got something for you."

He went into the hall and returned with a big leather-bound book. "Viola's diary," he said, plonking it on the table. "That should keep you going for a while."

After Granddad had gone, Caitlin pushed her plate aside and dragged the diary towards her. The dull leather cover was cracked and curling at the corners as though it had been left in the sun. Caitlin flipped it open and was soon devouring lines of flowing script that seemed to gallop from one side of the page to the other.

Jan 14th 1952

Visited Mrs Turkington today. She lost baby Joshua just before Christmas, at six months old. He had been a healthy boy. No problems with birth but developed colic. Mrs T. said from the time she began using Dewars', Joshua's health declined. The doctors were puzzled and treated him for recurring bacterial infections. Mrs T. is devastated. She carries so much guilt. Nobody can give her any answers about the death of her baby.

Caitlin moved to the comfort of the sofa. Her gaze travelled down to the next entry.

Jan 16th

I can hardly write this I am so angry. Three babies now. My suspicions about Dewars' are growing. All three babies: Joshua (6 mths), Reuben (3 mths) and Laura (15 mths), had been given Dewars' Tummy Tamer for colic. All died within weeks. It has to be the tonic. Why are health authorities not acting? It is 3 a.m. I can't sleep. How many more deaths will it take?

Just as Caitlin was turning the page, there was a knock on the door. She peered through the window first, as Granddad had taught her. It was Mrs Lusk from next door.

"Hello," said Caitlin, as she slid the door open.

"Hello, dear," said Mrs Lusk, peering around Caitlin. "Is he home?"

"He's at the supermarket," said Caitlin. "Can I help?"

Mrs Lusk looked anxious and tugged at a jade pendant around her crinkly neck. "Well, ah . . . I wanted to borrow his wheelbarrow. He usually—"

"I'm sure I can find it," said Caitlin. She pursed

her lips and scanned the back garden. "Um, now where?"

"It's all right, dear," said Mrs Lusk, waving her hand. "I'll come back later."

"No, it's okay," said Caitlin. "It must be in the garage." She grabbed the roller door key off the hook in the kitchen and skipped down the steps to join Mrs Lusk.

"I don't want to put you to any trouble, dear."

"No problem," Caitlin smiled. She pushed up the roller door and, sure enough, there was a red wheelbarrow leaning against the back wall. Caitlin wheeled it down the driveway and into Mrs Lusk's garden and was given a chocolate brownie for her trouble.

Back at Granddad's she was just reaching up to close the garage door when something caught her eye. Still on tiptoes, her fingers curled around the door handle . . . she froze. There, just visible behind a sheet of wallboard was the polythene package the policeman had delivered to her home two weeks before. Caitlin released the handle and lowered herself onto her heels. She walked slowly back into the garage, dragged the ungainly bundle out from behind the wallboard and stood staring at it. She started to sway, and steadied herself against the wall, waiting for the moment to pass. She opened her eyes. The polythene was tightly bound with tape so she grabbed some pruning shears and snipped it free.

Released from its body bag, the bike looked

smaller and less significant than Caitlin remembered. She breathed deeply as another wave of dizziness overcame her. She blinked hard and looked the bike over. The frame was pretty much intact, the blue paintwork barely scratched, but where the handlebars should have been, was a blunt stem of sheared metal. The fractured handlebars were still attached by thick black cables. Caitlin traced her finger across the fractured stem and yelped as a metal fragment pierced her skin. A trickle of blood leaked out and she sucked it. She spun the front wheel, which turned freely.

Caitlin wondered how an impact strong enough to snap off the handlebars hadn't buckled the wheel. She was still pondering this when she heard a car turn into the drive. Seconds later Granddad was advancing towards her, his footsteps heavy, his eyebrows a solid line of fury. "Can't turn my back for a moment, can I," he thundered.

"I was just—" Caitlin spluttered.

"I know what you were doing," he said, propelling her out of the garage.

Caitlin scurried up the steps and into the house. She sat quietly by the window watching her grandfather toss a paint-spattered throw over the bike, then yank the garage door down so hard that it quivered long after he walked away.

Caitlin swallowed, and went to help unload the groceries. She carried two bags from the car, put them on the bench then went into the dining room.

She sat, staring blindly at her maths workbook, wishing her granddad would say something but he just kept putting the groceries away in stony silence.

After a while, a hot chocolate appeared beside her and Granddad pulled up a chair. Caitlin put her pencil down but couldn't meet his eyes. "Why do you have to go upsetting yourself like that?" he said softly.

Caitlin shrugged and concentrated on the lace tablecloth, her eyes brimming.

Granddad picked up her protractor and began flexing it between his thick fingers. "Look, I know it's hard," he said, "but we can't change what happened." Caitlin nodded. "We have to move on."

Caitlin sniffed and took a sip of the hot chocolate. "But the bike . . ." she ventured, in a small voice. "It was . . . there was something wrong with it."

Granddad sighed and laid the protractor flat on the table. "And how're you going to prove that?" Caitlin shrugged. "Trust me love, it's just not worth it."

He got up, walked over to the window and stared into the distance. "I did enough of that when your grandmother died. Couldn't sleep, couldn't think. What if I'd been home that night? What if I'd made her go to the doctor when she had that. . . dizzy thing . . . the week before? What if? What if? But you know what?" He turned to face Caitlin. "Didn't change anything did it? Didn't bring her back."

Caitlin shifted in her chair. "It's rough, love, but what has happened has happened."

Caitlin looked down. A tear plopped on to the tablecloth. She felt her granddad's hand on her shoulder, a gentle squeeze, "C'mon, better get you home. She'll be wondering where you've got to."

CHAPTER NINE

The lift doors opened into the busy concourse of Southgate shopping mall. Saturday shoppers with weekend faces zigzagged across the vast, glass-domed atrium, past a Roman-style fountain with three plaster mermaids spouting water from their rosebud mouths. Potted palms in huge, blue-glazed containers imposed their tropical presence and, outside the entrance to a toyshop, a huge brown bear with a basket of sweets was attracting children like a magnet.

"This is scary," said Caitlin's mum, as the lift doors closed behind them.

"You'll be right," said Caitlin, feeling far from confident herself.

She'd been blown away when her mother said casually on Thursday night, "Let's go the mall on Saturday. She said she badly needed some new clothes and Caitlin could look for some winter tops.

Caitlin had felt both excited, because it was the first time her mother had actually wanted to go out, and anxious, for the same reason.

They'd got a taxi-van to the mall. The driver, recommended by Sonya, was friendly enough in a brisk kind of way, but it still shocked Caitlin to see her mother helplessly hoisted into the back of the vehicle. Sonya had reassured Caitlin when she'd admitted she was nervous about the outing. "You'll be fine," she said. "Just take it slowly."

Caitlin took a deep breath. "Right," she said, to the back of her mother's head. "Are you flying solo?"

"Yes," said Rita, pushing herself forward. "Just don't walk too fast."

Caitlin felt self-conscious ambling along next to her mother. She was tempted to pull her hood over her head but then she felt bad for even thinking that.

They made slow progress, competing with prams and shoppers drifting about like wayward sheep. Weaving their way through a crowd watching a kids' talent contest, they noticed a woman striding toward them. "Celia, from my photography class," Mum hissed, as the bird-like blonde strode up.

"Oh Rita, you poor dear," Celia trilled, causing nearby shoppers to gape curiously. "I heard about your . . . um . . . My goodness, aren't you doing well, out and about so soon." Caitlin fumed as the woman went on in the same tone, stooping to talk to her mother, the way you might to a small child.

"This is Caitlin, my daughter," Caitlin heard her mother say, far too politely, she thought.

The woman flashed Caitlin a sickly smile. "Aren't you a good girl, taking Mum out?" Caitlin felt her cheeks begin to burn. "So, you must come round," Celia was gushing. "Oh no, the stairs. Forgot about that. You'd never get up them." She looked around, as if for an escape route. "Um . . . anyway . . . we'll do something . . ." She was about to deliver an air kiss when Caitlin grabbed the wheelchair and began to move off. Celia jumped aside and raised her hand in a limp wave.

Caitlin!" said her mother, glancing over her shoulder. "That was a bit rude."

"Well, what about her?" Caitlin grumbled. "You'd think you'd lost a million brain cells as well as the use of your legs."

They headed, rather too fast for Rita's comfort, to Go Girl, Caitlin's favourite clothing shop. "I'll just wait outside," Rita said. "I won't fit in there."

Relieved, Caitlin pecked her mum on the cheek and disappeared into the pulsating pink interior. The place was full of young girls, midriffs bared above wide-studded belts, trawling through the latest fashions. Caitlin appeared at the door a couple of times holding up a top for her mother's approval. She eventually emerged with a happy smile and a carry bag, which she slung over the handles of the wheelchair.

Next they headed for the department store where Rita wanted to buy some underwear. The crowded racks of lingerie presented a new challenge as Caitlin tried to weave between them. For her mother, down below the level of most of the display stands, it was worse. She was swiped in the face by knickers and nighties and at one stage a bra got caught in her hair.

"Ow!" she yelled, as Caitlin screeched to a stop. They both started laughing as Caitlin fumbled to untangle the bra. Other shoppers started looking over to see what the fuss was about.

"I'm going to wet my pants," said Caitlin, jiggling on the spot.

"At least you *know* when you've wet yours," said her mother, wistfully.

Caitlin snorted and earned a stern look from a lady with a grey bob, who was testing the elastic in a pair of large knickers. Caitlin swung the chair around sharply and headed for the toilets.

"Let go," chided her mother. "I can do it myself." But Caitlin wasn't listening. She propelled the chair over the polished floor and through the food court, causing diners with laden trays to jump sideways and small children to reach for the hand of the nearest adult. She almost overshot the corridor to the toilets so she made an exaggerated sound like the screeching of brakes, tipped the wheelchair back on its wheels and spun around. Her mother gripped the seat with both hands. She opened her mouth to say something, but ended up just shaking her head.

As she waited for her mother, Caitlin reapplied

lip-gloss and teased the taps, the sort that automatically turn on when you put your hands underneath. "Haven't fallen down there, have you?" she called cheekily to her mother, aware it was the first time since she left the hospital that she'd used a toilet away from home.

Caitlin studied her reflection and raked her fingers through her hair. She inspected her tongue, imagining how a gold stud might look. She turned her back to the mirror and continued to wait. On the wall, next to a tampon dispenser, an ugly germ with bulbous eyes leered out of a poster saying: *Been shopping? You've got enough to carry without germs. Wash your hands!*

Caitlin thought of the school toilets and felt suddenly angry, comparing this gleaming place with what the kids at school had to put up with. She heard a door open and her mother pushed her way out of the cubicle. "Sorry," she said, smiling wearily. "Let's find some coffee."

They made their way back to the food court but it was right on lunchtime and the place was packed. "On second thoughts," Mum said, looking suddenly pale, "let's go home."

Caitlin felt relieved. She was tired of the noise, the obstacles, silly people and the constant stares. To make matters worse, she'd caught sight of Ella Peebles and her friends in the middle of a sea of cluttered tables. As she headed for the lifts, her mother coasting wearily beside her, Caitlin could feel their eyes burning like laser beams into her back.

"Talk about shop till you drop," said Mum, five minutes after they arrived home. She yawned. "I'm going to have a nap."

"What about coffee?" asked Caitlin.

"Maybe later. Don't think I've got the energy to hold a cup right now." Caitlin helped her mum onto the bed, pulled the curtains and returned to the lounge where she turned her attention to the 'Go Girl' bag. She spent the next hour on the phone telling Olivia about her purchases and how mad she was with Ella Peebles and company. "They just stared," she said. "So rude! I am so going to say something on Monday." Even as she said it, Caitlin knew she wouldn't.

About an hour later, Caitlin was watching a movie when she heard a thump in her mother's bedroom. She jumped up, sending Skoota flying, and sprinted down the hallway. She gasped as she went into the room to see her mother lying on her back besides the bed. "Missed the blimmin' thing," she said rolling over and easing herself onto her elbows. "Mustn't have had the brake on."

"Whoops," said Caitlin, guiltily. She stood rooted to the spot, not sure what to do. She made several awkward attempts to lift her mother back into the chair but it was no use.

"Better call Granddad," suggested her mother.

Caitlin dashed around in circles for a few

seconds then rushed to the kitchen to get the phone. Her fingers drummed on the kitchen bench as Granddad's phone continued to ring. She dialled Sonya's mobile, and was relieved to hear it answered immediately.

"I'll be there as soon as I can," said Sonya briskly. "Just make her comfortable."

Caitlin rushed back to the bedroom and packed pillows under her mother's upper body.

"Can't say it hasn't been an eventful day," Rita said, trying to ease Caitlin's obvious distress. A while later they heard a car in the drive.

"Legless at four on a Saturday afternoon," joked Sonya, striding into the room. Rita smiled but Caitlin didn't think the comment was very 'appropriate', as her teacher, Mrs Bowman, would say. She watched her mother loop her arms around Sonya's neck as she expertly eased her back into her chair.

"You know, you should think about doing some gym work," said Sonya, "so you can get yourself into the chair if this ever happens again."

"Mmmm," said Rita, looking sheepishly at her daughter. "You're not the first to suggest that."

CHAPTER TEN

"You should call him," said Caitlin, as she and Rita were preparing dinner.

"Maybe."

"Do it!"

"Bossy britches."

Caitlin lifted the lid of a steaming saucepan and dropped in a handful of spaghetti. The water rose over the top and hissed angrily on the hotplate.

"Careful," said her mum, peering up at the bench.

"It's sweet," said Caitlin, lowering the heat. "So – when are you going to do it?"

"Not that easy," said Mum, stripping a basil plant of most of its foliage.

"Why?"

"What is this? Twenty questions?"

"Could be a hundred if you keep on not answering."

Rita sighed. "Oh, I don't know. I just don't want him to think he has to stick around."

"His choice."

"That's it though, isn't it? He probably thinks he has no choice. He just stays out of guilt. Pass me the chopping board."

"Here you go. There's a bit of squashed something on the side."

"Where?"

"There."

"Oh. Right. Yick. You know . . . we hardly knew each other before this happened." *Chop, chop, chop.* "Not like he owes me anything." *Chop, chop, chop.*

"So?"

"Here, you can put this in. Careful."

Caitlin took the chopping board and scraped the diced herbs into a pot of thick tomato sauce. "Chill, Mum," she said, stirring the herbs in with a wooden spoon, "He might want to hang around."

"Yeah, right. Out of Pity?"

"Noooo! Good grief, Mum!"

"Set the table. There's a good girl."

Up in her room, Caitlin was running out of excuses for not working on her speech. She'd painted her toenails, scored several goals by dribbling the hockey ball around her messy floor and slamming it into a shoebox lying on its side under the window.

She'd plucked a dead African violet out of its bone-dry container and hurled it in the rubbish bin, and sent several text messages, to which she hadn't had one reply. She sighed, jiggled herself into a comfortable position on her bed and opened an old exercise book.

A few seconds later she was nibbling the pen, staring at a blank page and cursing Brooke for putting her name forward for the school council. She chucked the pen at the wall, got off the bed, turned in a circle, and sat down again. Every time she thought about the speech, her tummy closed in on itself like an irritated shellfish.

Caitlin sighed and reached for Aunt Viola's diary. She opened it and began to read:

Jan 20th

Spent an hour today trying to get Mr Tompkins to print my story. He is worried Dewars' lawyers will sue the Courier. He says I need to get more proof. Ten babies dead! What more does he want? I can't stand by and let this go on. I have to do something.

Caitlin read the words in a voice that was becoming familiar. She studied the photos of Aunt Viola again and smiled at the 'don't mess with me' eyes and the chin thrust forward to the camera. Just then her phone beeped.

Wat u up 2? It was Olivia.

Da stewpd speech

Wat speech?

Skool council!

Sux

I no. I cud kill Brooke.

Yeh.

GTG Mum's bellowing

K bye

Caitlin tossed her phone aside and reluctantly returned to her speech. She was munching on her pen and inspecting a rough piece of skin on her big toe, when an idea popped into her head. Why hadn't she thought of it before? Skoota leapt up beside her and gave a fishy-breathed yawn. Caitlin patted him distractedly as her pen began to fly across the page.

At 10pm Caitlin heard the television switch off and her mother come through to the living room where Caitlin was now working on the computer.

"You still going?" she said, yawning. "What are you doing?"

"Speech."

"Well, it's time you were in bed."

"Mum, did you know that there are hundreds of diseases that can lurk on taps in public toilets, and –

ooh this is so gross – when you flush, bugs and things in the toilet bowl are sort of sprayed into the air."

Mum screwed up her face. "I think I'd rather not know all that."

You should," said Caitlin, with an air of superiority. "We all should."

~

CAITLIN SAT in class feeling sick. Craig Watters was up the front talking about the need for more equitable gender balance on the school council. Mrs Bowman had to ask him to stop after five minutes so she could explain to the bewildered faces of his classmates, what he was talking about. "Craig thinks there are too many girls on the council," she'd said, nodding to Craig to continue. Some people sighed. Others slumped in their seats. Craig produced all sorts of graphs and diagrams (obviously borrowed from his dad) about equal opportunity strategies in local government. Finally, he gathered up his props and sat down.

"Ella," said Mrs Bowman with an expectant look on her face. Caitlin shifted in her seat as Ella Peebles, sleek ponytail bobbing, marched up to the front of the class. "Environment is everything," Ella declared, eyeballing the front row . . . and then she seemed to forget what followed. She looked panic-stricken for a moment then plunged her hand into the pocket of her white jacket with the faux fur collar and pulled out some cue cards. "Environment is everything," she repeated, less confidently, "which is why our school needs more flower-beds and landscaping . . ."

"Er, duh!" whispered Olivia leaning toward Caitlin. "I can see where this is heading." Ella's parents owned the local garden centre and were already making heaps of money out of supplying the school's gardening supplies.

Ella got through her speech and gathered up her catalogues of flowering plants and landscape designs. Mrs Bowman looked disappointed as Ella bobbed back to her seat and Caitlin took her place.

Caitlin scanned the class and her knees turned to jelly. Everybody was looking at her expectantly but her voice seemed to have free-fallen to the bottom of her stomach.

"Caitlin?" coaxed Mrs Bowman.

Caitlin looked over the heads of her classmates to a row of papier-mâché masks displayed on the back wall. The faces, some grotesque and leery, others goofy and clown-like, seemed to mock her as their features swam in and out of focus. Caitlin blinked and shifted her feet. She looked across at Mrs Bowman, who nodded encouragingly. Caitlin opened her mouth then shut it again.

The class jiggled restlessly and someone sniggered.

Caitlin's eyes swivelled back to the masks and lingered on one of a woman with pink cheeks and a piercing stare. The features slowly began rearranging themselves, the bright colours faded to black and white. Caitlin recognized the familiar tilt of the head, the defiant thrust of the chin and the eyes, egging her on. She squared her shoulders and cleared her throat.

"We have a serious problem in this school," she said steadily, "that's threatening our health and breaching our rights to a safe environment . . ."

All Caitlin was aware of was the cheering of her classmates. Her face was hot, and the cue cards, to which she hadn't referred once, were scrunched in a ball in her sweaty fist.

"Go Caitlin!" yelled Brooke. The boys started drumming their feet.

"Well!" said Mrs Bowman, almost as flushed as Caitlin. "Looks like you're the new class councillor."

~

GRANDDAD WAS at the gate to meet Caitlin after school and take her to hockey. "Well?" he asked as they pulled away. "How'd the speech go?"

"All right."

"Just all right?"

"Good, I suppose."

"For heaven's sake, Caitlin. This is like pulling teeth. Did you get class councillor?"

"Yep."

"Great!" said Granddad, thumping the steering wheel. He looked across at Caitlin. "Isn't it?"

"S'pose."

"Excellent, love. Good on you."

Caitlin shrugged and tugged at some loose threads on her sweatshirt.

~

AFTER HOCKEY PRACTICE they called into the fish and chip shop. Caitlin stayed in the car while Granddad went inside to place their order. She was playing hangman on her cellphone when she suddenly remembered that the shop where Granddad had bought her mother's bike was just around the corner. Caitlin peered through the steamy window of the fish and chip shop. She could see Granddad sitting on a bench seat, engrossed in a magazine, so she quietly slipped out of the car. She walked briskly past a row of shops, their buttoned-down frontages illuminated by the sickly glow of fluorescent lights. A chip packet skidded across the gum-spattered pavement, carried by a sudden gust of wind.

Caitlin thought back to the day two years ago when they'd gone to the shop. It was the week before Christmas and Granddad had seen the bikes in an advertising flyer that arrived in the letterbox. *Quality Bikes, Special Christmas Shipment* it had said. Caitlin remembered he'd been a bit suspicious at first. Couldn't believe he could pick up a decent bike for her mother so cheap. When he saw them, though, he was quite impressed.

"Won't get cheaper than that, mate," the shop owner had told them. She remembered the man unchaining a bike and suggesting Caitlin try it out. After a wobbly sweep of the car park she gave Granddad the thumbs up. He'd gone home very pleased with himself, Mum's Christmas present sticking out the back of his little hatchback

When Caitlin reached the shop she found it empty. A steel grille was pulled down over the window but through the narrow openings she could see the carpet littered with packaging material and price tags. A cash register sat on the counter and a card on the window said 'For Lease' and gave a phone number. Caitlin didn't have a pen but, as she hurried back to the car, she kept saying the number over and over in her head.

As she rounded the corner, she could see Granddad standing on the pavement, looking up and down the street, a steaming bundle in his hand.

"Sorry," said Caitlin. "Needed a phone card." On the way home she tore a piece of paper from the fish and chips package and scribbled down the phone number.

CHAPTER ELEVEN

It was dark when they turned into Caitlin's driveway, the car windows misted up and the car smelling of fish and chips. Granddad headed for the kitchen while Caitlin dumped her schoolbag and hockey gear and headed down the hallway.

"Mum!" she yelled. "Where are you?" She found her mother sitting in the lounge in the semi-darkness. "Hi," she said from the doorway.

"Hiya," said her mother. "What's new?"

"Got on the council."

"Excellent."

"Hmm."

"So they liked the toilet speech?"

"I guess."

"Good one, love."

She reached out and squeezed Caitlin's hand.

"What's up?" Caitlin asked.

"Nothing."

"Why are you sitting in the dark?"

Her mother shrugged. "No reason. Is that fish and chips I can smell?"

Just at that moment, Granddad yelled, "Come and get it!"

Caitlin followed her mother as she eased herself down the passageway.

"Did you hear about clever clogs here?" asked Granddad, plonking some tomato sauce on the table.

"Yeah," said Mum. "Good. Very good."

Something in her tone made Granddad look up. He examined his daughter's face. "How 'bout you? What did you get up to today?" There was a pause.

"Peter came round." said Mum, pulling paper napkins out of a drawer.

Granddad's hand hovered and stopped over a piece of battered fish. "From work?"

"Yeah."

What did *he* want?"

Caitlin's mother sighed deeply. "Well . . . he said they're having to *review* things."

"Oh yeah," said Granddad. Caitlin could see a tiny pulse begin in his temple. "What's that supposed to mean?"

"I think we both know what," Rita said, reaching for some chips. "He was very apologetic."

"I bet he was," said Granddad tearing a piece of fish in two.

"What?" asked Caitlin.

"Aw, nothing love," said her mother.

"What?"

"Huh. Just the modern corporate culture kicking people when they're down," growled Granddad.

"What?" demanded Caitlin, looking from one face to the other.

Her mother sighed and turned to Caitlin. "I'm not going to be working at Pinehaven much longer."

"They can't do that," said Caitlin, noisily squeezing the last of the sauce out of the bottle.

"They can do what they blimmin' well like," said Granddad, snatching the empty container out of Caitlin's hand and flinging it at the rubbish bin.

Caitlin found it hard to concentrate on her homework, thinking about her mum losing her job. She'd worked at Pinehaven for as long as Caitlin could remember. When she was small, Mum would sometimes take her to work. She remembered the floral carpet of the sunny day room, gravy-brown stockings, tugs of war with walking sticks, and soft sugary jubes offered by creepy, freckled hands. Caitlin bit hard on her pencil and closed her eyes. She couldn't imagine her mum without Pinehaven and she couldn't imagine the residents at Pinehaven without her mum.

Later, when Caitlin went down to the laundry to get her PE shirt from the drying rack, she heard voices in the kitchen. She lingered for a while and listened. She heard Granddad say, "It's sitting in the bank doing nothing. For goodness' sake . . ." She couldn't quite hear her mother's reply but Granddad's voice rose. "You can't raise that girl on a disability benefit."

"We'll get by," she heard her mother say. There was an exasperated sigh from Granddad. "C'mon Rita, let me help. Just till you get back on your feet." There'd been an awkward silence then they both started laughing. As she scuttled unseen out of the laundry, Caitlin glimpsed an embrace between father and daughter. She tiptoed upstairs.

Apart from thinking about her mother, Caitlin was also finding it hard to concentrate on her homework because of the racket Skoota was making. The big marmalade cat was on her dresser swiping noisily at ping-pong balls in the fish bowl. He'd stared so pathetically into the empty bowl after Finn died that Caitlin had put the balls in to amuse him. Now she was wondering whether it had been such a good idea.

"Knock it off Skoota," she yelled, but Skoota just turned his fluffy bum to her and continued. "Right," she said, flouncing off the bed and advancing towards him. As she reached out to grab him, Skoota swiped at Caitlin's hand. She jerked it away and knocked the fish bowl onto the floor. The first bounce didn't break it but the rebound against the dresser did. The glass, still covered in green scum, divided itself into three jagged pieces that now rocked gently on the floorboards. Skoota, eyes wide, and fluffed up like a cartoon cat, thumped onto the floor and scampered out the bedroom door. The intercom crackled.

"What was that?"

"Fish bowl."

"Broken?"

"Yup."

"How?"

"Skoota."

"Mmmm. He just streaked through here like a rocket. Be careful cleaning it up."

"Yes, MOTHER."

Caitlin went downstairs and got some newspaper. She went back to her room and was carefully laying the jagged glass onto the sheets when a headline near the top of the page caught her eye.

Bike Crash Ends Tour

Promising jazz pianist Peter Lee has had to postpone his international tour after a cycling accident in which he broke both arms. Lee, 19, underwent surgery last night to repair two badly broken wrists and a dislocated shoulder. His manager wouldn't be drawn on what the injuries could mean to his future career.

Details of the accident are unclear but it's believed no other vehicles were involved. A paramedic who attended the accident told the Gazette *it appeared Lee had gone over the handlebars, possibly after hitting a pothole or curb. "The bike's in bits," he said, "so he must have hit something pretty hard."*

Caitlin gaped at the paper . . . she shifted two jagged pieces of glass aside, tore the story out and tucked it in the back of her exercise book.

Next morning, as she was cycling down the road, Caitlin was surprised to see Phil coming the other way. She waved out and he slowed and pulled over. Caitlin pushed her bike across the road as Phil's window slid down.

"Hi," she said, shyly.

"How's it going?" said Phil.

"Good."

Caitlin didn't want to ask him if he was going to her place, in case he wasn't, but he saved her the trouble. "Just calling in to see your mum."

"Oh," said Caitlin. "Are you?"

"She called me," Phil added, quickly.

"Okay," said Caitlin

"Think she might be going to give the gym a try."

"Great." Caitlin unclipped her helmet and took it off, feeling suddenly self-conscious. She flossed her hair with her fingers.

"How is she?" asked Phil.

"She fell out of the chair the other day."

"God. Really?" said Phil, looking worried.

"Mmm. She was okay . . . just couldn't get back in."

"No."

"I tried to . . ."

"You'd never be able to . . . "

"Lift her. No," said Caitlin. She looked down

and scuffed her rubber soles on the rough roadway. A car whizzed by and she squeezed closer to Phil's vehicle.

"Did you ever find a receipt for that bike?" Phil asked. Caitlin shook her head. "Granddad would have it probably but he's . . ."

"Wanting to move on? Yeah I know."

Caitlin thought about telling Phil about the newspaper story but she decided against it. "Better get going," she said.

"Oh, right," said Phil. "I can give you a ride if you want. Throw your bike in the back."

"No, it's okay . . . thanks," said Caitlin putting her helmet back on. "Bye."

"Take care," said Phil as she wobbled off. She glanced back to see his SUV swing into her driveway.

CHAPTER TWELVE

Giving up her lunch hour to go to the school council meeting wasn't Caitlin's idea of fun. She didn't know anyone else in the room except Liam Marsden, whose presence, for some reason, just made her feel even more nervous. The meeting was being held in the new library, a large open-plan space that swallowed up the school's modest collection of books and screamed out for more. The building, a gleaming monument to the power of fundraising, featured angled wooden ceilings and alternating glossy yellow and blue panels that broke up the vast space that still smelled of polyurethane and the new carpet.

The eight new councillors, four girls and four boys, shuffled restlessly, sneaking glances at each other as they waited for the appointed teacher to chair the meeting.

Mr Gifkins eventually swept into the room, a roll

of papers under his arm and a mug of coffee in the other hand.

"No drinks in here, Mr Gifkins," came a shrill voice from behind a shelf of books. A grey, curly head on a long, flexible neck extended like a periscope above the shelves. Mrs Weavers, the school librarian. She fixed Mr Gifkins with a menacing stare. To the amusement of the students, Mr Gifkins went scarlet and lowered the mug under the desk. Mrs Weavers continued to stare at him like a vigilant ostrich, until he strode out the door and returned empty-handed. Two girls stifled giggles behind their notepads while other students grabbed books from the nearest shelf and pretended to thumb through them. Liam Marsden grinned and flicked his eyebrows at Caitlin. She smiled and rubbed at a stain on her top.

"Right," said Mr Gifkins, loosening his collar and tossing a resentful glance at the last sighted position of Mrs Weavers. "I . . . ah . . . declare the first meeting of the new school council open."

The first thing the new councillors had to do was to introduce themselves and explain the issue that had gained them a place on the council. A girl with a thin face and dark plaits said the food in the tuck shop was 'nutritionally deficient'.

Mr Gifkins, who looked as though he lived on nutritionally deficient food, looked unconvinced and moved on. "Next," he said.

A pale boy with blond hair, crunchy with gel, said the hockey turf needed re-surfacing. This was met with "ah ha" from Mr Gifkins, who noted something in a tattered green diary. Then he nodded at Liam.

Caitlin watched Liam get up and tug down his jersey. He stooped self-consciously and chewed his lip as he flicked through a grimy exercise book with dog-eared pages. Caitlin noticed for the first time how his thick, dark hair curled around his ears and at the nape of his neck.

"Um . . ." He giggled and looked around the table. "The school computers, sir," he said. "They suck." There was a ripple of laughter.

"Suck?" said Mr Gifkins, raising his eye-brows.

"Yes sir. They do."

"How?"

"Well," said Liam, looking as though he didn't know where to start, "they take about half an hour to start up, they don't have enough RAM, they run ancient software and freeze all the time." Around the table, several people nodded vigorously in agreement.

Mr Gifkins frowned. "Well, don't hold back, Liam."

Liam missed the joke and took up the invitation to continue. "And," he said, "there are different versions of Windows, no network connections, missing mouses – I mean mice – and too many seriously old computers."

"Yes, yes, I think I've got the picture," said Mr Gifkins, irritably. "I'll take it up with the Board."

Liam sat down. The exercise book, which he'd rolled tightly as he spoke, now wouldn't sit flat on the desk and he smiled at Caitlin as he thumped it.

Caitlin tried to return the smile but her face had seized up. It was her turn now and she was feeling very queasy. As she got to her feet her heart began hammering and her tongue seemed to swell in her mouth. Mr Gifkins cleared his throat and slowly drummed his fingers on his open diary. "Caitlin?"

Caitlin forced herself to breathe. She looked down at her notes and said. "The school toilets are a health hazard."

"Ah, yes, the toilet girl," said Mr Gifkins, with a mocking smile. Everybody laughed.

"They stink," Caitlin continued.

"Well, that's a surprise," said Mr Gifkins, scanning his audience for some support. "School toilets that stink."

Caitlin blushed and looked down. "There's no hot water or soap," she said in a quivery voice. "The towel dispensers are bro—"

"And why do you think that is?" blurted Mr Gifkins, his toad-like eyes bulging with enquiry. "Vandals," he said, before Caitlin could answer. "Vandals. Wreck everything in the school."

People shifted uncomfortably. Someone coughed. Caitlin swallowed. "They're unhygienic," she said.

"I daresay they are," said Mr Gifkins. "Not nice people at all." He beamed at his own joke and was honoured with a couple of snorts of laughter from around the table.

Caitlin's heart was racing, her cheeks burning. She mouthed like a stranded fish.

"Listen, my dear," Mr Gifkins said, in a patronising tone. "I admire your passion – I do – but it's a bit of a lost cause, this toilet thing." He wrote something in his diary. "I'll certainly mention it to the Board but they've heard it all before." He smiled tightly. "Best concentrate on things we can change. Okay?"

The bell rang and Mr Gifkins snapped his diary shut. "Same time next week?" he said, heading for the door.

Caitlin was left standing, her fists balled in fury, as chairs scraped around her.

"The school council sucks," Caitlin complained to her friends later, as they squished wet clay through their fingers in art.

"Why?" asked Brooke.

"It's just the biggest waste of time." Caitlin didn't tell them about how she'd been totally shamed by Mr Gifkins and that she blubbed behind the hedge on the playing fields for half an hour before she'd returned to class.

"I wouldn't want to do it," said Olivia.

"Exactly," said Caitlin, shooting Brooke an accusatory look.

Caitlin sat on her bed listening to the radio and picking cat hairs out of a mohair throw. She could go down and start dinner but her mum would call her soon enough, when she needed help. "Not the right attitude," she could hear Granddad say. "Better to offer before you're asked."

Caitlin frowned. None of her friends had to do half the stuff she did. She got off the bed and thrust her hands into the pockets of her track pants. Her fingers found the scrap of paper from the fish and chip shop . . .

Later, after she'd grudgingly done the washing up, Caitlin grabbed the phone and stabbed out the number.

The man who answered the mobile spoke in a gruff, heavily accented voice. Caitlin explained she was looking for the man who'd run the bike and toy shop in the Glenville shopping centre.

"'E's friend of yours?" the man asked suspiciously.

"No," said Caitlin. "I . . . we bought something from him."

"Not my problem," said the man.

"I know," said Caitlin, "I know. It's just that I need to find—"

"Me too," said the man.

"Pardon?" said Caitlin.

"'E owe me rent, dat bugga."

"Oh," said Caitlin. "Does he?"

"'Ee's bad news."

"Okay."

"I have a lot of customers ring about dat guy. Unhappy customers."

"Well . . ."

"'E's did a runner."

"All right," said Caitlin.

"Eet not my problem."

"But . . ."

"If yous find 'im, you call me. Eh? 'E cause me big trouble."

"Okay," said Caitlin.

Click

"Bye."

CHAPTER THIRTEEN

Next day at school, a strange thing happened. During library session, Mrs Weavers, who was cataloguing books at the front desk, kept smiling at Caitlin. Once, she even winked. "Mrs Weavers is seriously freaking me out," Caitlin whispered to Olivia. "She keeps smiling at me."

"Maybe she's a lezzo," said Olivia.

Caitlin kicked her under the table and for the rest of the session she tried to avoid looking over at Mrs Weavers.

Then, as Caitlin was leaving, the librarian said, "Caitlin – could I have a word?"

"Look out," hissed Olivia, as Caitlin peeled away from the queue heading for the door. She approached Mrs Weavers' desk. "I just wanted to congratulate you on your speech to the school council the other day," said Mrs Weavers.

"Oh, right," said Caitlin, relieved.

"You were absolutely right with what you said about the school toilets and you should be listened to."

"Thanks," said Caitlin, smiling.

Mrs Weavers opened her desk drawer and took out a large envelope. "There's some material in here you might find useful . . . for your campaign."

"Campaign?" said Caitlin.

"You will be taking it further, won't you?" she said, as though there could be no shred of doubt.

"But Mr Gifkins said the Board wouldn't do anything," said Caitlin, anxious to get going.

"That oaf," said Mrs Weavers. "Sorry, but what would he know?"

Caitlin had to suppress a giggle. "But—"

"You go for it, and make someone accountable," said Mrs Weavers firmly. "You've got to."

Later that evening Caitlin sat in her room pouting as she recalled the conversation. Mrs Weavers had no right to boss her into doing something about the toilets. She'd done her best, hadn't she? And had been shamed in front of the whole school council. If Mrs Weavers was so bothered, Caitlin thought, she could do something herself. She spent the rest of the evening playing computer games and texting Olivia and Brooke. She didn't help her mum clean up the kitchen, which she felt bad about, but she told herself she needed a night off. It had been a very stressful week.

On Saturday morning Granddad arrived to take Caitlin to hockey. She'd slept in and was running late. He was not happy. "For goodness' sake, Caitlin," he said, "the game's at ten. You knew that!"

"I can't help it if she didn't wake me," Caitlin said.

"*She* is your mother – and don't talk like that."

"I did wake her," said Rita, pouring her father a coffee.

"I won't have time for that, love."

"She must've gone back to sleep."

"Where are my shin pads?"

"I don't know. Wherever you put them."

"Come on, Caitlin. We'll be struggling to get there on time."

"Not my fault."

"Whose is it then?"

"Have you had any breakfast?" asked Mum

"Don't want any."

"You've got to eat something."

"See ya."

"Here, take a banana and some yoghurt."

"Grrr."

"Bye . . . good luck."

SLAM!

Before they pulled out of the driveway, the lecture had begun. It was all about being more organised and responsible 'under the circumstances'.

About helping Mum more, being more understanding, blah blah blah.

Caitlin knew Granddad was right and she knew better than to argue. She said "yes" and "I know" about a million times before they arrived at the hockey grounds. Caitlin's team was just running on but she'd already been subbed because they didn't think she was coming. By the time Caitlin jogged onto the turf, fifteen minutes into the game, her team was 4 – 0 down. In the end they got thrashed, ten goals to one.

That afternoon Caitlin went to the movies with Olivia and Brooke. It was Olivia's birthday and they were all staying over at her house. Caitlin went through the entire contents of her wardrobe (which didn't take long) trying to decide what to wear. She finally settled on her new green top, camouflage cargos with a wide studded belt, and sneakers. Olivia wore jeans, a long pink-and-white-striped top, and white boots she'd got for her birthday. Brooke had on sand-coloured pants, a black top over a white T-shirt and black sneakers.

The trio gathered in the foyer that served four movie theatres. The place smelled of popcorn and cheap body spray and was full of teenagers, mostly girls, eyeing each other and chatting self-consciously. Caitlin pushed her belt tightly onto her hips and ran her tongue over her braces. "C'mon," she said, tugging Olivia by the arm. "Let's get in the queue."

"I'm having popcorn – jumbo," said Brooke, digging in her handbag.

"Same," said Olivia. "What about you, Caitlin?"

Caitlin was distracted. She'd caught a glimpse of Ella Peebles and her friends, heading up the stairs. "Caitlin?"

"Huh?"

"What are you having? We're getting popcorn."

"Ah, ice cream," said Caitlin. "Chocolate dip."

"Maybe I will too," said Brooke frowning. "Except I usually end up with chocolate all over my pants."

"Yeah – looks like poo," said Olivia.

"Ew!" said Caitlin. "Do you mind?"

"Well it does! Little chocolate bits fall on your lap, then they melt in the dark. Looks like you've—"

"Yes," said Caitlin. "I get the picture. I'll have popcorn too."

The movie was funny, in a silly kind of way. It was about two city teenagers who go on holiday in a country town, get bored and decide to go on a crime spree. At one stage they rob the local bank and make their getaway on horseback. Neither of them can ride and they're bouncing up and down on the back of a horse with the money flying everywhere. Caitlin was really enjoying the movie until the hapless robbers come across some trail bikes, leaning against a fence, and decide to take them.

From the time they were kicked into life, Caitlin began to feel sick. The screaming whine pierced her eardrums and she looked down at her lap. Beside her, Olivia and Brooke were laughing their heads off.

Caitlin shut her eyes but the dizziness intensified so she was forced to open them. That was a big mistake. Just as she did, the camera moved around so that it was filming over the handlebars of the motorbike. It was as if Caitlin was in the driving seat and there was no escape.

She clenched her fists as the ground began sliding beneath her in a dizzying blur. Her heart was hammering, she could hardly breathe. Just when she felt she couldn't take any more, the bike launched into mid-air. Caitlin's stomach did a massive flip and she groaned.

Olivia's alarmed face came into focus in the flickering darkness. "Caitlin?" The scene changed and Caitlin pulled herself to her feet and stumbled out to the rest room.

While Caitlin splashed her face in the hand basin, with Brooke and Olivia fussing around her, Ella Peebles and her two friends came in. It seemed the movie had finished.

"Hi," said Brooke, trying to sound friendly. Ella just nodded and fished in her bag, while her friends disappeared into cubicles.

"Cool movie, eh?" said Brooke.

Ella was smoothing a wand of expensive looking pink gloss across her lower lip. "I guess," she said lazily. "I saw it last holidays, flying back from LA."

"Right," said Brooke, blushing and picking an imaginary piece of fluff off her top.

Ella dragged her fingers through her glossy hair and gave her head a little shake. Seemingly happy with the result she turned her attention to Caitlin, who was dabbing her pale face with a paper towel. "Ooh, have you just puked?" she asked, screwing up her face. Caitlin couldn't be bothered replying.

"She's just not feeling great," volunteered Brooke.

"Ewww," said Ella, moving away. "That's what happens when you spend your time lurking in school toilets." Her two friends snorted loudly.

"Get lost," spat Olivia.

Ella pretended to be shocked. She clasped her heart-shaped pendant, and looked down at Olivia, who hardly reached her shoulder, even in her new boots. "Don't tell me *you're* a member of the toilet police as well" she smirked. Olivia blushed as Ella's friends giggled.

"As a matter of fact, she's not," said Caitlin, firing a screwed up paper towel at the rubbish bin, "but like me, she knows crap when she sees it." She nodded at the front of Ella's pants. Ella glanced down with a look of horror at the brown smudges on the front of her perfect white denims.

CHAPTER FOURTEEN

The deadline for her 1950s project was getting close and Caitlin hadn't touched it for more than a week. With the rain pelting down outside and her mum in the gym, she decided she'd better get into it. She hauled out Aunt Viola's diary, found her place, and started reading.

Feb 2nd

I've finally convinced Mr Tompkins to publish my story. The laboratory results on the tonic came back positive for high levels of bacteria and health authorities have a warrant to close the factory. We publish on Friday. I don't think any of it would have happened if I hadn't got myself arrested.

Arrested! Caitlin thumbed through the newspaper clippings and eventually found it.

> **Journalist Arrested**
> County Courier *journalist, Miss Viola Saunders, was arrested today after an incident outside Dewars' Factory in Alexander Street. In the pursuit of a story Miss Saunders presented herself at the factory at 9.30 a.m. demanding to speak to proprietor Arthur Dewar about matters that, for legal reasons, can't be revealed by this paper.*
>
> *A spokesman for Dewars' Ltd said that Miss Saunders refused to leave when asked and had to be forcibly removed. After being escorted from the premises she is reported to have climbed onto the roof of a parked motor vehicle to address passersby about matters hitherto declared legally sensitive. Police arrested Miss Saunders at 2 p.m. She has been charged with wilful trespass and civil disorder.*

"Whoa, go Aunt Viola," Caitlin laughed to herself. She grabbed her phone and texted Brooke.

Guess wat? Im related 2 a criminal

Lol. Hu?

Great Aunt V

Wat she do?

Trespassed & stood on a car
Stood on a car??
Long story
Rains a bumma eh?
Yeah
Wat u doin?
Hmwk. U?
Cleaning my room
Bumma
cya
bye

Caitlin put her work aside and went downstairs for some food. Just as she strode into the kitchen, Phil's 4WD pulled into the drive. Through the rain-flecked window she watched him unload her mum's wheelchair, then go around and scoop her out of the passenger seat. She looked like a doll in Phil's arms, his smooth biceps hardly bulging with the effort of lowering her into the wheelchair. By the time they came through the door, Caitlin's head was buried in the fridge.

"Hiya," said Phil, following her mum into the kitchen.

"Hi," said Caitlin. "How was the gym?"

"Exhausting," said Mum, tucking a stray wisp of hair behind her ear. She nodded at Phil. "He's the trainer from hell."

"Moi?" said Phil, looking insulted. "We're just getting started."

There was an awkward silence. "Right," he said. "Better go. See ya Wednesday?"

"If that's okay?" said Mum.

Caitlin sighed. This strained politeness was almost harder to take than when her mum was being grumpy with Phil. After he'd gone, Caitlin said, "Why didn't you ask him to stay for coffee or something to eat?"

"He needs to get away. He has stuff to do."

"He told you that, did he?" asked Caitlin.

Her mother looked dangerously rattled. "Caitlin. Leave it please."

"Okay. Whatever."

Caitlin found it increasingly hard to pick her mother's mood. There were good days, when she seemed relaxed and she could get away with saying anything and other days when she had to weigh up everything that came out of her mouth. It wasn't helped by the fact that the job at Pinehaven had officially come to an end, her mother was now on a disability benefit and money was in short supply. Granddad would breeze in every Friday with a box of groceries and veges from his garden. Last week, a new toaster appeared on the kitchen bench. Caitlin's mum had frowned and told Granddad off. He'd just said, "It was on sale for next to nothing. For goodness' sake, if I can't buy you a present occasionally, it's a pretty poor show."

Back up in her room, fortified by two plates of nachos, Caitlin hauled her schoolbag onto her bed and began probing its dark recesses for her green highlighter. She found the envelope Mrs Weavers had given her and was about to throw it aside when curiosity got the better of her, so she picked it up and opened it. Inside was a photocopy of a newspaper article headed: *'Lifting the Lid on School Toilets'*. Caitlin huffed and was about to shove it back but her eyes were already scanning the first few sentences.

Five minutes on she was totally engrossed and getting angrier by the minute. Her highlighter had slashed bright green through four key sentences.

70 per cent of students don't use school toilets because of lack of hygiene, bullying and vandalism.

Many kids suffer serious health problems because they won't go to the toilet at school.

Bugs that cause vomiting and diarrhoea spread rapidly in our schools because of the substandard state of school toilets.

Many school Boards treat toilet maintenance and hygiene as a low priority.

Caitlin frowned. If things were so bad, why hadn't something been done? She picked up the article and looked at the date. It was three years old. It had been published in a national newspaper three years ago yet nothing had changed. Why not? She remembered Mr Gifkins' dismissive tone: ". . . bit of a lost cause. . . the Board's heard it all before." A truly awful image of Mr Gifkins sitting on the toilet came into Caitlin's mind. She shuddered and shook her head. It might be a different story if he had to use the filthy school toilets, she thought.

She sat pondering this for a moment and realised she'd chewed the top of her new glittery pen. As she flung the mangled pen at her overflowing rubbish basket, she felt a new appreciation for Mrs Weavers. "She's right," she said to Skoota, who looked totally unmoved. "People have to be *made* to care."

~

AT LUNCHTIME THE NEXT DAY, in a corner of the school library, six pupils were huddled in earnest conversation. In front of them was a proposed plan of action, tabled by Caitlin Nove, School Councillor, Room 5. It had taken some organisation to get the council members to attend the special meeting (two hadn't bothered showing up) but support for Caitlin's action plan was gaining momentum.

"But don't all schools have this problem?" asked a thin-faced girl called Lucy Rajpal.

"Doesn't make it right," said Caitlin.

"But it's not the school's fault if vandals keep wrecking the toilets."

Caitlin opened her mouth but was beaten by Liam Marsden. "That's just an excuse," he said, with a passion Caitlin found quite exhilarating.

"Yeah," she said, and if the toilets were nicer – cleaner – maybe people wouldn't trash them."

"And they *can* be made more vandal proof," said Ani Epiha. "That's what they did at my old school."

"It's not right that we don't have soap," said Mitchell Trantor, "'specially when the health nurse keeps telling us about the importance of washing your hands."

"Imagine teachers having to put up with toilets like ours," said someone else.

"Well, they wouldn't, would they?" said Liam. "That's the whole point."

After a little more discussion, a vote was taken and Caitlin's plan for direct action was unanimously passed.

"Thanks for letting us use the library," Caitlin called to Mrs Weavers, as she went out the door, "and for the photocopying."

"No problem, dear," said a gravelly voice from behind a bookshelf. "More than happy to help."

"I can do the flyers if you want," said Liam, catching up with Caitlin as she strode into the sunlight. Caitlin stopped and squinted up at him. The sun was behind him and made him look taller, bigger somehow. His hazel eyes grew wider for a moment, inviting an answer.

"Cool, thanks," she said, feeling herself blush. "That would be good because our printer's stuffed."

Liam nodded. A yawning silence stretched between them. "Ah . . . what – what's wrong with it?" he stammered.

"Dunno," said Caitlin, scrabbling for an impressive explanation. "The . . . ah . . . light thingy keeps blinking and it won't . . . um . . . print."

"Hmm," frowned Liam. "Have you turned it off and on?"

"Doesn't make any difference," said Caitlin. Liam pursed his lips and looked thoughtful. Caitlin noticed for the first time how long his eyelashes were.

"I can check it out for you sometime," he said. Caitlin realized Liam was waiting for a response and she had no idea what he'd just said. "If you want, I can look at it," he repeated.

"Cool," said Caitlin. "That'd be awesome."

"Okay."

"Right," said Caitlin, jiggling.

"See ya," said Liam, with a shy smile.

"See ya," replied Caitlin, striding off and colliding with the post of a netball hoop.

CHAPTER FIFTEEN

Over the next week some subversive activity began under the radar of unsuspecting teachers at Dunstan Road School. Students huddled together chatting about the upcoming action and cell-phones buzzed with updates.

The fifth of June started like any other school day but it soon became clear that something extremely odd was going on. The principal's secretary, Mrs Dreever, discovered two Year 7 girls in the staff toilets in the administration block. They took no notice when she tried to shoo them out. Mr Gaskin, newspaper under his arm, strolled into the technology staff toilet to find a queue of boys snaking out the door. A packed staffroom gaped in disbelief at 8.45 a.m. when half a dozen girls marched in and disappeared into the new staffroom toilet. All over the school, as quickly as the culprits were cleared, another group appeared.

When forced to explain themselves, pupils refused to speak. Instead they handed teachers a leaflet that said:

"We are protesting over the appalling state of the toilets we are forced to use at this school. We believe they breach our basic human rights to cleanliness, privacy and dignity. This is a health and safety issue and we want assurances the Board and staff will take our concerns seriously."

And in small print underneath:

(This action has been authorized by the School Council.)

With the staff toilets overrun with pupils, teachers were forced to use the students'. Mrs Heggarty had to stand guard outside a cubicle occupied by Miss Walters because there was no lock on the door. Mr Gaskin practically gagged as he entered the boys' toilets in B block. He certainly wasn't going to sit and read his newspaper in there! And Mr Darlington was caught short with no toilet paper in the hall toilets. All the teachers searched in vain for soap and came out shaking their freezing hands or wiping them on their clothing.

By 9.30, the harassed principal, Wally Walters, was forced to call an emergency assembly.

"He looks wild," whispered Olivia. "Totally," said Brooke.

"Well," said Caitlin, "he'd better be careful."

"Why?" asked Olivia.

Caitlin gestured to the back of the hall. "The media are here."

~

The story in the *Courier* next day caused a huge stir. Health and education officials visited the school, Board members were summoned, and teachers were extra fidgety.

Mr Walters, who looked as though he hadn't slept for a week, appeared on the evening news, saying he was grateful to the school council for highlighting a serious health and safety issue. "While I don't condone wholesale disobedience," he said, "in this case, pupils have acted responsibly to bring a serious matter to our attention."

"I should hope so!" said Caitlin, scratching Skoota under the chin.

"Wow," said Mum. "You sure got them listening."

"Yeah, we did."

"Good for you."

"We're onto the tuck shop now," said Caitlin.

Her mother narrowed her eyes. "Really?" she said, a hint of alarm in her voice.

"Possibly," said Caitlin. "The food is rubbish."

"I hope you're spending as much time on your schoolwork as you are on stirring," said Granddad, as they headed for the vet on Saturday morning. Skoota had been fighting again and had an abscess on his face.

"It's not 'stirring'," said Caitlin indignantly, "and we were right."

"I'm not saying you weren't – but you've got to think about where your priorities lie."

"Eh?"

"You've got other things to worry about." Caitlin rolled her eyes and sank down in her seat. "Don't remind me," she said under her breath.

"Pardon?" For once, she was glad of Granddad's deafness.

Nothing," she said.

They drove on in silence with Skoota mewing and clawing at the bars of his cage.

ON MONDAY CAITLIN arrived home to find a note on the pad by the telephone. It was in Mum's writing and it said:

Hi Love

Did you get my text? Have an appointment about the car. Sonya's taken me. Sorry, forgot to tell you. Open can of soup if you're hungry.

Megan Ryan from the Courier called. Asked if you could call her.

Mince for tea. Can you chop some veges plse. Whatever's in the fridge. Should be home by 5.

Love Mum

PS. Skoota's still in the laundry. He hates that bucket. Give him one of those yellow pills with his dinner – and can you clean out his tray please? Sorry.

Caitlin sighed and checked her mobile. She had got the text but hadn't replied because she was out of credit and didn't want to ask her mum for the money to top it up.

She went into the laundry and screwed up her face. The 'deodorizing' kitty litter didn't seem to be working. Skoota looked miserable, standing under the window with a plastic bucket framing his indignant face.

"Poor puss," crooned Caitlin, emptying the soiled tray into a large plastic rubbish bag. She replaced the litter, spooned some food into his bowl and pushed half a pill into a chunk of jellymeat.

She stood back and watched Skoota trying to manoeuvre himself into a position where he could eat. "Aw, unfair," she said, going and tilting the dish towards him. Skoota gave her an evil glare and began eating. Caitlin slowly walked out and closed the door.

She knew she should get into her homework but

was curious about the call from the Courier. She looked up the phone number, then grabbed Mum's note from the hall table, took it through to the kitchen and picked up the phone.

She was put through to the editorial department where the phone was answered by a cheery voice that said. "Hi, Megan here."

Caitlin took a big breath. "Hi. It's Caitlin. Caitlin Nove from Dunstan Road School."

"Hey, Caitlin. How are you doing?"

"Good."

"Thanks for calling back."

"That's okay."

"Hey, you guys really made your school sit up and take notice, eh? Good on you." Megan went on to explain how she was writing a feature story about school councils and the growing influence of pupil power in modern education. She said she'd like to meet Caitlin and talk about how she came up with the idea of taking direct action over the toilets.

"It wasn't just me," said Caitlin.

"That's not what I heard," said Megan, with a throaty giggle. "Just kidding. Hey, look it's nothing heavy. Honestly."

"Right."

"Hey, you should be proud of yourself. When I was at school, I wouldn't have said boo to a goose. Not that we had gooses . . . I mean geese . . . at school."

Caitlin laughed politely.

"I sure make up for it now."

"Mmm."

"Anyway, sorry. When can we meet up?"

Caitlin said it would probably be best if Megan didn't come to school because Mr Walters was a bit sensitive about reporters.

"Aw, totally," said Megan. "I bet he is," she said, giggling again.

"You could come to my place," said Caitlin, uncertainly.

"Cool, sure, no problem. When?"

"I've got hockey practice tomorrow."

"Hey, a hockey girl. I used to play hockey."

"Okay."

"What position are you?"

"Left half," said Caitlin.

"Cool – I was mostly left right out."

"Ha."

"Just kidding. Actually, I loved my hockey."

"Cool."

"Anyway, so tomorrow's out. Okay . . . what about Thursday?"

Caitlin thought for a minute. "Yep."

"Thursday okay?"

"Should be."

"Cool. What time?"

"I'm usually home by four," said Caitlin. "Well, just after." She gave Megan the address.

"Excellent," said Megan. "I'll see you then."

CHAPTER SIXTEEN

Caitlin didn't really miss having a dad because she didn't know what it was like to have one, but sometimes, like tonight, when she was around her friends' fathers, she felt envious. Kirsty's dad was taking them to hockey practice. He'd taken over as coach because Mrs Keyes had left to have a baby.

"Thought I'd try you on the wing tonight, Caitlin," he said, looking at her in the rear vision mirror. "You've definitely got the speed."

"Okay," said Caitlin, trying to sound positive. She didn't like playing out of her usual position but she understood Kirsty's dad was trying to make his mark as new coach. She studied his face in the mirror as he drove and tried to imagine what her own dad would look like now. All she really knew about him was that he was nineteen when he was killed and that he and her mum were planning their wedding when he died. Once, she'd come across some photos in her mother's dresser. There was one of Dad and Mum dressed up for the school ball and another of them on a beach. They looked so young.

The little information Caitlin had about her father had come from her grandma. Her mum clammed up whenever her father was mentioned and so did Granddad. All Caitlin knew was that Kevin – that was her dad's name – and Granddad didn't get on. Grandma told her that Granddad could never forgive Kevin for getting her mum pregnant while she was still at school. Now that she knew how babies came about, Caitlin thought that was unfair. Grandma said that after Kevin died, her mother and Granddad didn't talk for ages. Caitlin didn't know how they got started again. She wished she'd asked Grandma more about it but now it was too late.

"How's your mum?" asked Kirsty's dad, as they stopped at the lights.

Caitlin thought about the question for a moment. She felt like saying: *She's in a wheelchair, she can't walk, she can't run. She can't do anything much. She has no control over her bowel or bladder. She's lost her job and she's worried sick about money. How the hell do you think she is?* Instead she just said, "She's fine, thanks."

AT 4.10 ON Thursday afternoon the doorbell rang.

Caitlin was in her room trying to decide whether to wear her jeans or her cargoes. She'd already taken each one on and off four times. She settled for her cargoes but then realized there was a grass stain down the front so she chucked them in the corner and pulled on her jeans. She frowned as she studied herself in the full-length mirror, then tugged up the zip, smoothed down her thighs and stomped out the door.

By the time she got downstairs Megan was in the lounge talking to her mother. Although she was sitting, Caitlin could see she was quite tall. She had reddish curly hair, glasses and braces which was surprising because she must have been in her 20s. She was wearing black pants and boots with seriously pointy toes, a cream ribbed jersey and a black jacket. Caitlin stood at the door until they both looked her way.

"Caitlin, I presume?" said the tall girl, standing up and extending her hand.

Hi," said Caitlin shyly.

Mum offered Megan a cup of tea or coffee but she said she was fine. "Okay," she said, wheeling herself out of the room. "I'll be on the computer."

Megan told Caitlin about the story she was doing and said she'd spoken to kids from other schools that have strong student councils. "But," she said, smiling, "none of them are quite as . . . um . . . active as yours."

Caitlin blushed.

"No, no," said Megan. "Don't get me wrong. I

think it's great. It took courage to do what you did." She said she'd heard that the health department was looking at drafting new regulations for school toilets because of what had happened at Dunstan Road School.

"True?" said Caitlin. "Wow!"

"Yeah. Straight up. You should be very proud of yourself."

Caitlin blushed again and stared at the carpet.

They talked for a bit longer then Megan closed her notebook – but she seemed reluctant to go. "Your mum's lovely," she said. "Must be tough being . . you know . ."

"Yeah," said Caitlin.

Megan shuffled to the edge of the sofa. "Do you mind me asking what happened?"

"It was a bike accident," said Caitlin. She didn't mind telling Megan the story because she could see she wasn't just nosy but really interested. Her green eyes locked on Caitlin's as the story unfolded and she shook her head in disbelief.

"Oh no," she kept saying. "Oh no, that's awful."

Caitlin stopped short of mentioning anything about her suspicions about the bike but she could see Megan's mind working overtime. "So the handlebars *broke*?" Megan asked, frowning and cocking her head simultaneously. "That's odd." Caitlin just shrugged. "Holy-moley," said Megan, looking at her watch. "I better fly."

Caitlin got up and followed her to the door.

Much to Caitlin's surprise, Megan gave her a big hug. "I think you're cool," she said. "Take care."

"How'd it go?" said Rita as Caitlin wandered into the kitchen and scanned the pantry.

"Megan has braces," she said. "Weird, eh?

"S'pose," said her mum. "Guess there's no age limit, if you want perfect teeth."

"Would she have gone to university to be a journalist?"

"Don't know. Why?"

"Nothing. Just wondered." Caitlin extracted a jar of peanut butter and started eating it with a spoon.

"Caitlin!" scolded her mother. "I wish you wouldn't."

"Hardly any left. I'm just finishing it off."

Rita shook her head and looked at her daughter. "Would you like to be a journalist?"

Caitlin rolled her eyes. "Mum, I'm twelve years old. It's a bit early for planning the rest of my life."

"Sorry."

Caitlin worked the spoon around the inside of the jar, scraping up the last of the peanut butter. "How did Aunt Viola get to be a journalist? There wouldn't have been many women doing it in those days would there?"

"No. I think she just started writing . . . and got started that way."

"Mmm."

"I guess she must have had 'an enquiring mind'," said Mum. "Like someone else I know." Caitlin snorted. "Well," said Mum defensively, "you do have her genes."

Caitlin found a packet of crackers and stuffed two in her mouth. "Talking about jeans," she said, "look at these."

"Don't talk with your mouth full. What?"

"These. They're awful. I've had them for ages."

"What's wrong with them?"

"They're gross."

"Don't be silly. They're fine."

"Look."

"What?"

"Here," said Caitlin twisting to view her bottom. "See? They make me look deformed."

Mum laughed. "They don't."

Caitlin pouted and took another couple of crackers. "They so do," she said in a spray of cracker crumbs.

CHAPTER SEVENTEEN

Caitlin's glue stick glided across a small square of paper, down the sides, across the top and a dab in the middle for good measure. She lined the square of text in the centre of a blank sheet and carefully pressed it with her fingers. Below, in black felt tip, she wrote...

County Courier, June 1952

"There," she said to Skoota. The big cat narrowed his eyes and began delicately cleaning his curled paw. Caitlin flicked through the pages of the clear file and nodded approvingly. She especially liked the title page:

Viola Bridget Saunders 1912 to 1956

She'd photocopied and enlarged a photo of Aunt Viola and then gone over it with a thin black pen so it looked like a sketch. She was due to present her project to the class on Monday but there was a rather large piece of the jigsaw missing. Caitlin had noticed her aunt's diary finished abruptly on November 12th 1956 and there was no clue in the envelope of newspaper clippings to explain why or what had happened to her.

She got up and went downstairs. Her mother was in the dining room, plucking at a basket of clean laundry. "What happened to Aunt V?" asked Caitlin, flopping in a chair opposite her.

"Why?" asked her mum, pausing as she folded a towel.

"Duh . . . coz I need to know for my project," said Caitlin, rolling her eyes.

"Hey, watch the smart talk," Rita warned. She finished folding the towel and placed it on a pile. "She died . . . in a house fire."

Caitlin sat up. "Ohmigod . . . true? How come you never said?"

"You never asked."

"Oh, right." said Caitlin. "Well that figures."

THE NEXT DAY Caitlin showed Mrs Weavers her finished project.

"It's very good, dear," the librarian said, turning over the plastic sleeves and peering at the text. She stopped at a photo. "You know – you look a lot like her. The eyes."

"Hmm," said Caitlin. Mrs Weavers flicked back

to the title page and frowned. "1912 to 1956? She was only forty-odd . . . forty-four . . . when she died."

"I know. Sad eh?"

"What happened?"

"She died in a fire," said Caitlin. "At her home, apparently."

Mrs Weavers looked up. "So where's the report on that?"

"Huh?" said Caitlin.

"Well," said Mrs Weavers, "if she was that famous, there must been something written about her death, surely?"

Mrs Weavers was right, of course. Caitlin realised as soon as she said it. Aunt Viola was famous, and she worked for a paper so somewhere there would have been a story about her death – a story Mum and Granddad had conveniently forgotten to mention.

After school, Caitlin caught the bus into town and went to the library. Mrs Weavers told her the old newspaper records were kept on the first floor. She walked up to the information desk, where a young man with blond hair and acne looked up from his computer screen. "Hello, can I help?"

Caitlin explained that she needed to research some old newspapers and the man led her upstairs to a part of the library she'd never been to. Glass doors slid aside as they entered a room with long tables and cabinets full of labelled boxes.

"The records are stored on microfiche,"

explained the man. "You can view it on this reader." He pointed to a machine with a wide screen and some spools and sprockets on which to thread the film. "So, what were you after?"

"The *County Courier* around November 14th 1956," said Caitlin.

The young man unlocked a glass cabinet and plucked out a box. Inside was a roll of film, which he threaded into the machine and started scrolling though. "There you go," he said. "You should find what you're looking for here."

It took Caitlin a while to get a hang of the reader but soon she was confidently scrolling through metres of film, learning all sorts of things about life in the fifties. Eventually she found what she was looking for. A *County Courier* article dated November 15th 1956.

Fire Claims Life of Journalist

Police are investigating a fire that claimed the life of County Courier *journalist, Viola Saunders. Miss Saunders' remains were found in the charred wreckage of her home after an intense blaze that took the County Fire Service two hours to contain. It is not known how the fire started, in the early hours of Sunday morning, but police removed a petrol can from the porch.*

Miss Saunders, 44, was one of the country's most distinguished journalists, winning the Press Association's highest award for her work on the Dewars' baby tonic scandal.

County Courier *Editor, Edward Tompkins, says Miss Saunders was an exceptional journalist, who would leave no stone unturned in finding the truth. She was working on an investigation into the deaths of four coal miners at the Sheffield Valley Mine at the time of her death.*

Her funeral will be held in St Theresa's Church on Wednesday.

Caitlin was surprised to find her eyes welling with tears. She thought of the defiant young woman with the shy smile and electric hair. She fished in her pocket for a tissue and blew her nose as quietly as she could in the loud silence of the library. She focused again on the reader and scrolled down to another story.

Death of Journalist Remains a Mystery

Police have closed the investigation into a house fire, which claimed the life of

County Courier *journalist, Miss Viola Saunders, late last year.*

Miss Saunders died in a fierce fire that destroyed her home in Darling Road in the early hours of Sunday, November 14th. *Police believe an accelerant was used to start the fire, which completely gutted the small wooden bungalow.*

While police believe the blaze was suspicious, they say any evidence that may have helped them find the person or persons responsible, was destroyed in the fire.

"We have a charred petrol can, found on the porch, but little else to go on," said a police spokesman. "We have no choice but to close the file."

Police say they will re-open the case if any further evidence comes to light.

"Why didn't you tell me Aunt Viola was murdered?" said Caitlin, as soon as she arrived home.

Her mother was in the kitchen, grating a carrot on a board on her lap. She stopped and turned to Caitlin.

"It was never proven."

"I've seen the story, Mum. A petrol can – police investigation."

Well, we thought . . ."

"We?"

"Well . . . Granddad thought it would be better for you not to know."

"Jeez, Mum," growled Caitlin. "I'm not five."

"I know you're not, love, but—"

"I don't get you guys! You wanted me to study her for the stupid project, then you only tell me half the story!"

Mum sighed and put the board and grater on the bench. "Yeah, I guess . . ."

"Oh forget it," said Caitlin and flounced out of the kitchen.

~

It was late when Caitlin finally finished her project and proudly laid it on her desk. Before she went to bed she took Aunt Viola's photo out of the envelope and propped it against her bedside lamp. The glow of the lamp bathed the image in soft golden light. Caitlin shuddered as she imagined her fiery death. She lay studying the picture until a sleepy fog engulfed her. She turned out the light, rolled over and dreamt fitfully of riding her bike through a burning forest, keeping just ahead of the flames that flickered and crackled behind her.

Although Caitlin was totally shocked about what had happened to Aunt Viola, it had certainly added a bit of spice to her project. When she finally presented her work to the class, everybody was riveted.

"The cause of the fire was never found," she explained gravely at the end of her presentation, "but a charred petrol can was found in the porch." She paused for effect then snapped the big diary shut. Everybody jumped. Then she gathered up the photos and newspaper clippings and ambled back to her seat.

"Well, thank you, Caitlin," said Mrs Bowman, clutching at her neck chain. "Now, Craig . . . your talk's on . . . ah . . ." She looked down at her notes. ". . .your Uncle, the Borough Councillor who designed our town's water system?"

Everybody groaned and sank lower in their seats.

~

WITH HER PROJECT finally out of the way, Caitlin could concentrate on organising her birthday party, just two weeks away. The hardest thing with birthdays was deciding who not to invite. Her mum said she had to limit the list to ten. That wasn't going to be easy.

Caitlin hauled a lined refill out of her school-bag, and started making a list. The intercom buzzed. "Caitlin, phone," called her mum.

Caitlin grabbed the phone from the kitchen and sat on the stairs.

"Hiya," said a cheery voice. "Megan here – from the Courier."

"Hi," said Caitlin.

"Just thought you'd like to know the story's going to be in Saturday's paper. In the feature section."

"Awesome."

"What are you up to?"

"Aw, nothing much. Just planning my birthday."

"Cool, how old?"

"Thirteen."

"Ah, a stroppy teenager."

"Ha."

"Well, have a good one, and thanks for—"

"Hold on . . . Megan?"

"Yep."

"I just wondered . . . um ..."

"C'mon, spit it out."

"I ... there was a story in your paper ... about a month ago ... about a guy who had a bike accident ... he was a piano player or something?"

"Hmm, think I remember ... vaguely."

"Do you think ... could you . . .?"

"Get a copy for you? Not a problem," said Megan. "Woohoo, you're turning into quite the little investigator!"

"Ha. Nah, I just—"

"Hey, just kidding. Leave it with me."

Caitlin said goodbye and returned the phone to the kitchen, where her mum was sorting through a pile of bills, tapping on a calculator and frowning.

She looked up as Caitlin walked in. “What did Megan want?” she asked.

“She just rang to tell me the story’s going to be in the paper on Saturday.”

“That’s good.”

“Yeah,” said Caitlin coolly, though she felt really excited.

CHAPTER EIGHTEEN

Granddad turned up as usual on Friday night with takeaways, some things from his garden and a box of groceries.

"Dad," his daughter scolded. "I told you I can handle it."

"What?" said Granddad, his tufted eyebrows dancing. He winked at Caitlin. "So bossy, your mother." Caitlin smiled. She knew Granddad meant well but she could also see her mum's point of view. She needed to feel she could still provide for the two of them, although Caitlin noticed it was getting harder every day. She'd heard her on the phone to the bank earlier in the week. There'd also been talk about taking in a boarder. Caitlin didn't like the thought of that at all.

"How's the gym going?" asked Granddad, as he plonked the curry containers on the table.

"Good," said Mum, looking genuinely pleased. "Helping a lot." She flexed a bicep, which bulged impressively.

Caitlin and her grandfather whistled and exchanged satisfied glances.

Just as they were finishing dinner, there was a knock on the door. Caitlin went to answer it – and did a double take. It was Megan. Her cheeks were rosy and she was slightly breathless as she plucked off her gloves and reached in her pocket.

"I was just passing," she said, "and thought I'd drop this off." She waved a folded sheet of paper toward Caitlin. "Quite interesting," she said. "I think you'll find that previous accident was very similar to what happened to your Mum."

As Caitlin reached to take the paper, she heard a noise and turned around to see Granddad behind her. His face was like thunder. Megan must have picked up the vibes because she didn't stay long.

"Did I just put my foot in it?" she whispered.

"It's okay," Caitlin replied. "Granddad's just a bit . . . sensitive."

"Whoops." Megan winced. "Sorry."

The air was pretty tense when Megan left. Granddad didn't say a word but it was written all over his face. Caitlin knew she'd get the lecture on the way to hockey next morning.

Later, as she was composing her birthday invitation on the computer, her mum rolled up. "That's cool," she said as Caitlin centred some clipart of a birthday cake under pink lettering saying 'You are invited'. "I suppose I'd better think about food."

"We're having pizza," said Caitlin. "Bought ones."

"Sure?"

"Yep."

"Well, that's easy," said Mum, making no attempt to leave. Caitlin sensed that birthday food was the last thing on her mind. Out of the corner of her eye she saw her pluck a paperclip out of a little glass dish and begin fiddling with it. Caitlin continued experimenting with colours on the clipart. The blue was a bit overpowering, so she was trying yellow.

Finally, her mother spoke. "Love, I'm not sure it's wise to get Megan involved in our business."

Caitlin gripped the mouse tighter and felt her face heat up.

"Did Granddad say that?" she asked in a tight voice.

"No, I just think—"

"He did, didn't he?"

"He's worried about you."

"Why?"

"He's just concerned you're meddling in stuff . . . best left."

"And what do you think?"

"I don't know. I—"

Caitlin felt a flash of anger. "Why's he like that?"

"Like what?"

"A total control freak."

There was silence. Caitlin rotated the mouse in tight circles, sending the curser flying madly around the screen.

Her mother twisted and bent the paper clip. When she spoke again, her voice was softer. "Your dad would have been so proud of you," she said.

Caitlin snorted. "Mum, do you know how cheesy that sounds?" Her voice was shrill and disapproving. Under the desk her foot began bobbing crazily.

Her mother continued, as though she hadn't heard. "He was pretty feisty, your dad – and stubborn. Probably why he and your granddad didn't get on."

Caitlin didn't trust herself to say anything. She wanted to get up and run but another part of her craved the information her mother suddenly seemed willing to share.

"The night Kevin died," her mum continued, "he and your granddad had had a huge row . . . he took off in a temper."

Caitlin continued staring at the monitor. "What about?" she asked. Her voice sounded sulky, grudging.

"You, actually."

"Me?"

Her mother took a deep breath and looked out the window. "Granddad didn't want us to get married. Kevin was doing his best – he'd got himself a building apprenticeship – but it wasn't enough for your granddad. He was always going on at him." She seemed lost in thought for a moment, staring into the darkness outside.

Caitlin shifted in her seat. Her mother went on. "Kevin got fed up with it. He wanted us to get our own place." She sighed deeply. "Granddad wouldn't have a bar of it . . . we had you by then and we didn't have any money."

Caitlin slowly swivelled around to face her mum.

"Anyway," Rita continued, "he said no way were you going to leave his house. Kevin got really mad . . . it was awful. He pushed Granddad out of the way, took you from the cot and yelled at me to pack a bag."

"What did you do?"

"I didn't know what to do. I didn't want to have to choose. I had Kevin screaming in one ear and Dad in the other. I don't know . . . I just couldn't move. Anyway, next thing, Kevin just ran to the car, put you in the back and took off. Said he'd come back for me later." The hum of the computer filled the silence.

"So, what happened then?" Caitlin asked.

Her mother lifted her head. A shudder rocked her body and she wrapped her arms tightly across her chest. "We heard the crash. A truck came through the intersection . . . at the end of the street. The car went under. The front was . . . crushed. You were in the back."

They both sat in silence. Caitlin looked at her

mother. She looked pale and exhausted. "You were going to get married."

"Yeah." Rita gave a hollow laugh. "We were." She shook her head and sighed. "It wouldn't have worked."

"Why?"

"Oh, we were too young . . . and totally different. Your granddad could see that, and I think he was right."

"What happened after Kevin died?"

"I left, that night, with you. Went to live with Kevin's mother."

"My other Gran?"

"Yeah. She died, when you were about two. Never really got over Kevin's death."

"What about Grandma and Granddad?"

"I didn't see Dad for nearly five years, though I used to secretly meet Mum. He never knew."

"How did you start talking again?"

"I suppose I got older and started to see his point of view. Only daughter – pregnant at seventeen. Can't have been easy for him. I s'pose he was only trying to protect me – and you." She reached out to stroke Caitlin's cheek but she ducked away and her mother smiled weakly. "It broke his heart when I took you away. He felt he'd lost both of us. Now, maybe you can understand why he's so . . . protective."

Caitlin folded her arms and looked away. Her mother smiled "He doesn't mean to—"

"Mum. I get it. Okay?" Caitlin turned back to the computer. The screen shimmered and she blinked to clear her eyes. After she was sure her mother had gone, she slumped, her hands over her face, her shoulders shaking silently.

CHAPTER NINETEEN

Caitlin stood outside the school gates peering up and down the road at the cars coming and going in the chaotic after-school rush. Megan said she'd be there just after 3.30 but so far Caitlin hadn't spotted her battered – and very noisy – yellow car. While she was waiting, she texted her mum.

Going for a hot choc, she said, which wasn't exactly a lie, because she and her friends often did. It's just that this afternoon the rendezvous was with Megan and Peter Lee, the jazz pianist whom Megan had tracked down

At 3.45 Megan's car roared into view and if the car itself didn't attract enough attention, Megan sure did. There she was, her red curly head out the window, waving and yelling "Oi, Caitlin! Caitlin!"

Caitlin scurried across the road and tried the front passenger door. It wouldn't open. "Oops," said

Megan, leaning over and jiggling the lock. "Try again."

In the end, Caitlin had to get in the back door then climb over to the front seat. Impatient drivers tooted their horns and Megan accelerated away before Caitlin was quite ready, causing her to tumble sideways in the seat. "Whoops, sorry," she giggled with a flash of braces. "How you doing?"

"Good," said Caitlin, recovering and searching for the seatbelt.

Five minutes later the pair walked into a café called Lillie's. Megan was wearing a pair of pale denim jeans that Caitlin thought looked really cool, and a khaki T-shirt that said 'Warrior Woman' on the front. Caitlin felt self-conscious in her school uniform and was glad when Megan headed for a dark alcove in the corner. At the counter, a girl with a nose stud was chewing gum and operating a coffee machine that spat and hissed as she worked the levers.

"Been busy?" asked Megan, smiling brightly.

"Kind of," said Caitlin.

"What have you been up to?" asked Megan, flicking a quick glance toward the door.

"Mostly working on a school project," said Caitlin. "But I've finished now."

"Good for you," said Megan. "What was it about?"

"My great aunt."

"Cool. What'd she do?"

Caitlin laughed nervously. She wasn't sure she wanted to get into Aunt Viola's life story with Megan, but it was impossible to resist Megan's obvious interest. "She was a journalist," said Caitlin, embarrassed, although she wasn't quite sure why.

"Ah ha!" said Megan. "A journalist, eh? Must've been one fine woman!"

Caitlin blushed but Megan, as always, had more questions. "What was her name?"

Caitlin cleared her throat. "Viola. Viola Saunders."

Megan's arms dropped like lead weights, her eyes lit up. "No way?"

"Yeah," said Caitlin with a nervous giggle.

"Ohmigod," said Megan. The girl at the counter peered over at them. "We studied her at journalism school. There's a picture of her on the wall of our office!"

Now it was Caitlin's turn to react. "Really?" she said, not absolutely sure Megan wasn't having her on.

"Yeah. She worked for the *Courier*, right? Well it was the *County Courier* back then."

"Yes, she—"

"Seriously, and she was your aunt? She was, like, totally famous. She did that story about . . . um . . ."

"Dewars' Baby Tonic," said Caitlin.

"That's the one," said Megan, her eyes wide. "Gawd, she was—"

Just then a slim Asian man walked through the door, casts on both arms. "This could be our man," said Megan, getting up. "That's why I'm a journalist," she whispered. "I'm so damn sharp!"

Caitlin laughed. She liked Megan. Her sense of humour reminded her of her mother – before the accident.

"Peter?" said Megan, offering her hand. The man smiled brightly and then extended a rigid arm.

"Oops, sorry," said Megan as she gently grasped the tips of his fingers.

Peter Lee laughed. "That's okay, no problem." He looked over Megan's shoulder at Caitlin.

"And this is Caitlin," said Megan, sliding into her seat. "Her mum . . . you know, I told you on the phone."

"Hello, Caitlin," said the man. "Nice to meet you."

The trio ordered hot drinks and Megan bought Caitlin and herself a brownie.

While Megan and Peter talked, Caitlin studied the man. He looked to be in his mid-twenties, with a friendly face and well-cut, shiny black hair, in which was nestled a pair of expensive looking sunglasses. He was cocking his head and nodding intently as he listened to Megan. Caitlin was looking at the casts that encased both his arms from just below the elbow to the tips of his fingers, when she suddenly became aware that a question was being directed at her.

"Wasn't it, Caitlin?" Megan repeated.

"Sorry, what?" said Caitlin, blinking.

"Your mum. It was about eight months ago?"

"Yes," said Caitlin, "it was."

Megan asked Caitlin to explain about her mother's accident. As she did, Peter Lee nodded gravely and occasionally shook his head in disbelief. When Caitlin had finished, he sat back, looking suddenly pale.

"So – tell us what happened to you," said Megan, spooning some coffee froth into her mouth.

Peter took a deep breath and closed his eyes, as though the recollection itself was painful. He said he was staying with a friend, a fellow musician, who was a keen cyclist. He'd suggested they go for a bike ride in a local park. Peter said he wasn't keen because he hadn't ridden much but the friend persuaded him and he borrowed a bike belonging to the man's young son.

"I was very . . ." He moved his plastered arm through the air in a zigzag motion.

"Wobbly?" suggested Megan.

"Yes," he said flashing his fine white teeth, "very wobbly, but then I start to enjoy it . . . it was good to be having some fresh air."

Caitlin and Megan nodded in agreement. Peter plucked a sugar straw out of a bowl on the table and began flexing it back and forward. "My friend wanted to go to Settler's Reserve." He raised his eyebrows and Megan nodded to indicate that they knew where he meant. He said they hadn't even got to the reserve when the accident happened. "There's a big hill," he explained, tilting his forearm downwards like a slide, although it looked more like a ski jump in the white cast, "and the entrance to the park is at the bottom."

"Yip, know where you mean," said Megan, taking a bite of her brownie.

"I was behind my friend going down the hill but I start to go too fast so I try to ..." He curled the tips of his fingers in a gripping action.

"Brake," encouraged Megan.

"Yes," Peter nodded. "I'm going very fast down this hill and I pull on the ..." He flexed his fingers again, "the thing . . . and suddenly the handlebar break."

Caitlin swallowed. She looked up from the tabletop into Peter Lee's face.

"Next, I am flying like this . . ." He lifted his plastered arms above his head in a wide-handed dive. ". . . over the top and kabush!"

"Ohmigod," said Megan, swallowing

"Do you still have the bike?" asked Caitlin, suddenly forgetting her shyness.

Peter reached down into a backpack and hauled something out. "Some of it," he said, laying a set of handlebars on the table. "This is the bit that snap off."

CHAPTER TWENTY

Caitlin couldn't take her eyes off the fractured handlebars, thick black cables sprouting from them like severed arteries. She remembered her mother's, sheared off in exactly the same place, dangling from the bike frame. She felt a tightness grip her chest and had to make a conscious effort to breathe. She looked up at Peter.

"Where did your friend get the bike?" she asked through almost clenched teeth.

"I thought you would ask," he said with a smile and began, with some difficulty, probing his hip pocket. Eventually he extracted a scrap of paper and handed it to Caitlin. It was headed 'International Importers' and there was a PO box number.

"Well, that's a start," said Megan, patting Caitlin's forearm.

After Peter Lee left, Megan turned to Caitlin. "So, Miss Detective, what are you going to do now?"

"Don't know," Caitlin shrugged. Her eyes darted away and her fingers began drumming the table.

Megan's eyes softened. "It's your Granddad, isn't it?"

Caitlin shrugged again. Her cheeks were flushed.

Megan began chasing brownie crumbs around her plate. "Yeah, it's tricky. For sure." She licked the crumbs off her fingers. "But you've got to work out what's important to you."

"Mmmm," said Caitlin, pushing her finger through some spilt sugar.

They sat in silence for a moment, then Megan said, "Wonder what your aunt would've done?"

"Aunt V?" Caitlin smiled and put on a plummy voice. "She'd say, 'this is truly and utterly appalling'."

"Reckon she would," said Megan. "If she knew about this, she'd be out to kick some serious butt."

"Yeah," said Caitlin, "she would."

~

IT WAS WELL after six when Caitlin got home. Granddad's car was in the driveway, hitched to a trailer full of garden clippings.

"Hi," said Caitlin as she walked into the kitchen. Granddad had his back to her. He was emptying the dishwasher. On a chopping board on the bench sat a pile of diced vegetables. "Finally," he said, turning to Caitlin. "Where have you been?"

"I went for a hot chocolate," said Caitlin, worried

her face would betray her. "Mum knew."

"Who with?" Granddad asked coldly.

Caitlin swallowed. "My friends," she said. Well, it didn't feel like a total lie. Megan had become her friend.

"Where's Mum?" asked Caitlin, anxious to change the subject.

"At the gym," said Granddad. He was briskly unloading the cutlery and firing it noisily into a drawer.

Caitlin looked guiltily at the tidy kitchen, the dinner sitting prepared on the bench. "Can I do anything?" she asked.

"There's nothing left to do," said Granddad, batting the drawer shut.

Mum and Phil eventually came home and Caitlin was pleased to hear Phil accept an invitation to stay for dinner. She thought her mum looked good, her cheeks were pink from her workout, and she was humming as she scanned a pile of advertising brochures lying on the bench.

"So, what have you been up to?" Phil asked Caitlin, as they tucked into fish cakes, chips and salad.

"Not much," said Caitlin. "Just school and stuff."

"Did you get that project finished?" he asked.

"Yeah, yeah, I did," said Caitlin.

"How'd it go down?"

"Great. Really good." She munched her salad thoughtfully. "Nobody else has a murdered journalist in their family, so it was good." Caitlin heard her mother cough. She glanced defiantly at Granddad but he just sat there eating in stony silence. Phil laughed nervously and glanced around the table.

"Yes," he said pushing his fork into a crumbed fish cake. "That sure would take some beating." The rest of the meal was eaten in tense silence. Caitlin was clearing the plates away when she heard her mother ask if anybody would like some strawberries and ice cream. Whoops. She knew she'd forgotten something.

"Um, there isn't any," she said. "I . . . um . . . didn't go to the shop."

"Caitlin," groaned her mother. "Honestly!"

Caitlin heard her Granddad sigh loudly and shake his head.

"I can go grab some," volunteered Phil.

"No, don't worry," said Mum. "We can do without it."

"Well, I can't," said Phil, grabbing his keys. "C'mon, Miss Memory-like-a-sieve, you can come with me."

Caitlin slid into the cab of Phil's vehicle. "Guess I'm in trouble – again."

"Mmm, your granddad didn't look too impressed."

"Well, Jeez," said Caitlin. "It's only a few groceries. Not the end of the world."

Phil smiled at Caitlin's scowling face."Right. So

what's it to be? Rocky Road or Orange Chocolate Chip?"

On the way back from the supermarket, Caitlin told Phil about meeting up with Peter Lee and the story of what happened to him. "Sheesh, is that right?" he said, looking genuinely interested. "And they snapped in the same place?"

"Exactly the same," said Caitlin. "He has a receipt." She dug in her pocket. "Here."

Phil glanced at the paper, then back at the road. "International Importers?" he said, screwing up his face. "Sounds a bit bogus."

"Bogus?"

"You know. Not exactly original, is it?"

"Yeah, I guess."

"Can I have this?"

"Sure."

Phil pushed the receipt into his shirt pocket. "I'll make a few calls," he said. "Let you know what I find."

~

On Saturday the crackle of the intercom woke Caitlin. Her mother's voice drifted through the mists of sleep. "Sorry, love . . . but I could do with some help down here."

Caitlin's eyes sprung open. She looked at the clock. 9.30! She tumbled out of bed, grabbed her dressing gown and stabbed the intercom button

"Coming."

Caitlin found her mother in the kitchen. The fridge was open and a milk carton lay on the floor, its contents seeping into a widening puddle.

"I just opened the door and it tumbled out," said Mum. "Next time push it further back, eh?"

Caitlin looked affronted. "Who said it was me?"

"Who had hot chocolate last thing?"

"Oh. Yeah," said Caitlin."Sorry." She scooped up the milk carton and mopped up the mess. As she returned the mop to the laundry she had to edge around her mother who was extracting a load from the washing machine.

"There's still a couple of socks and knickers in the back of there." She frowned. "Would you mind?"

"Yep, watch out," said Caitlin, squeezing in beside her. She dumped the smalls in the laundry basket and straightened up. She noticed for the first time that her mother was showered and dressed, and the smell of bacon wafted from the stove.

"How long have you been up?" asked Caitlin.

"Couple of hours," replied her mother. While her mum was doing her best to play it down, Caitlin knew she was making the effort to be as independent as possible. It was the first week they'd had to do without Sonya because the health board only supplied home help for six weeks and that time was up.

Caitlin was whisking up some pancakes when the phone rang. It was Phil. "I've been doing some checking," he said. "International Importers does exist. It is a registered company but I don't think it's the one we're after."

"How do you know?" asked Caitlin.

"Know what?"

"That it's not the one."

"Because it's an Asian food importer, based in Auckland. Brings in rice and stuff – no mention of bikes, toys or anything like that."

"Right," said Caitlin, fishing a fragment of eggshell out of the mixture.

"It's also been around since the eighties, so I think it's probably not connected."

"Right."

"The guy who brought in those bikes probably got a temporary import licence to bring in a stack of cheap stuff from Asia for Christmas. He's probably long gone."

"Mmmm."

"The PO box number doesn't check out either."

"Right."

"Sorry, kiddo. Not much help."

"Well, thanks anyway," said Caitlin. "Do you want to talk to Mum?"

Caitlin hurried up to the bedroom. Her mother was pushing herself around the bed, straightening the duvet. "I'll do that," Caitlin said, handing her the portable phone. "It's Phil." She went back to the kitchen to finish the pancakes.

A short time later her mother came into the

kitchen, her face lightly made up and her wet hair pulled back in a ponytail.

"Phew," she said, stretching her neck this way and that. "I'm knackered and the day hasn't even started."

Caitlin smiled. "Coffee's there," she said nodding towards the bench.

As she flipped pancakes, Caitlin felt her mother's eyes on her. "I feel so bad about you having to do all this," said her mum.

"Yeah," said Caitlin, scooping a pancake up with a fish slice and sliding it onto a tray in the oven. "You're a total pest." She glanced at her mother's fallen face. "Just kidding."

"Well," said Mum, opening the cupboard and taking out two plates. "Things are about to get a little easier."

"How?" asked Caitlin, closing the oven door.

"I get my new car next month."

"Definitely?" Caitlin asked, beaming widely.

Rita nodded.

"Sweet. What colour?"

Her mother laughed. "I don't know yet, but that's the least of my worries."

"Hey, you should so get lavender. That's so in."

"Whatever."

"Well, just don't get boring white, will you?" Mum shook her head. "No, seriously Mum. You can't get white."

CHAPTER TWENTY-ONE

Caitlin's pen twirled and looped a decorative daisy pattern on the top of her agenda paper as she listened to Liam Marsden addressing the school council. To be honest, she couldn't understand a word he was saying – it was a whole lot of techno-babble about computers, but it sure sounded impressive. She gazed at Liam, as he shifted from one foot to the other, reading from a fistful of crumpled papers. His school jersey, which was way too small, rode up his arms and the hem of his grey shirt peeped out the bottom of the stretched waistband. His olive face was set in concentration as he read.

". . .so that's what we'd need for a full system, which would allow us to network," he said, looking up from his notes. Mr Gifkins, looking slightly cross-eyed, nodded attentively and wrote something in his diary. Since the business over the school toilets, Caitlin noticed he'd begun to take council proceedings much more seriously. She'd heard from Mrs Weavers, who was a terrible gossip, that the principal had blamed Gifkins for the whole toilet thing getting out of hand and embarrassing the school.

Apart from meticulously recording everything, Mr Gifkins had also begun to treat Caitlin a bit like a live grenade, speaking very slowly to her as well as frequently and nervously asking, "And what do you think we should do about that, Caitlin?"

So far, as well as planning an upgrade of the toilets, the new school council had banned greasy and sugar-laden food from the tuck shop – not to everyone's satisfaction – and got the school bus service to run on time. Today, Liam was presenting some costings on upgrading the computer system.

"So," he concluded, "if we get the hardware through Ram Parts, rather than buying new, we can get the best deal." He sat down, swiped his fringe out of his eyes and smiled at Caitlin.

"Excellent," said Mr Gifkins, a nervous twitch pulling at the corners of his mouth. "Thanks for that, Liam. I'll uh . . . certainly take that to the Board."

The meeting ended and Caitlin was talking to Mrs Weavers at the front desk when she noticed Liam waiting near the door. When she glanced over he started reading the notice board. Mrs Weavers had called Caitlin over to ask about her mother. She had started to take a real interest in the goings-on in Caitlin's life and Caitlin had come to enjoy their frequent chats. She found Mrs Weavers' wrinkled face and intense sparkly eyes somehow comforting and she'd even got used to her overpowering musky perfume.

"Looks like someone wants to talk to you," said Mrs Weavers, nodding towards Liam.

"Yeah," said Caitlin, hesitating.

"Well," said Mrs Weavers, with a chuckle, "off you go."

As Caitlin approached, Liam turned towards her. "Did you get your printer sorted?" he asked.

"No," said Caitlin, blushing. "It's totally ancient. I think it's munted."

I could check it . . . if you want."

"Ummm . . ." said Caitlin, pushing the door when she should have pulled it. She groaned inwardly. Liam reached over her head and yanked the handle towards them. Caitlin stepped back and stood on his foot. "Sorry," she giggled, going scarlet.

"Ow," said Liam, hopping around in mock pain.

Outside, they both squinted in the sun. There was an awkward silence.

"Probably just needs resetting."

"Huh?"

"The printer," said Liam, tugging down his jersey. "I can come round if you want."

"Okay, that would be good," said Caitlin, not knowing what else to say.

"Right," said Liam.

"Right," said Caitlin, and they marched off in different directions.

When Caitlin checked her phone at lunch, there was a text from Megan.

Can u call me?

Caitlin was frustrated because she still didn't have any credit on her phone. She'd just have to wait till she got home. She was distractedly chewing a muesli bar when Brooke spoke to her. "So, what time on Saturday?"

"Huh?" said Caitlin, swallowing quickly. "Your party," said Brooke, frowning. "I so haven't got anything to wear."

"We're just hanging," said Caitlin.

"I know," said Brooke, "but I still—"

"Hey, let's dress up!" offered Olivia. "Have an eighties party. I could raid Mum's—"

"No!" yelled Caitlin and Brooke together. "All right, calm down, calm down – I didn't say we should turn up naked," said Olivia, sulkily.

"Well, it's my party," frowned Caitlin, "and we're not dressing up."

"Right," said Olivia, sniffing and poking her nose in the air. "So – what are you wearing?"

"I don't know yet," said Caitlin. "It's only Wednesday."

"Well, you have to tell us," said Brooke firmly.

"Whatever."

"What DVDs are we getting?" Olivia asked. Caitlin rolled her eyes. "Cinderella and Bambi," she said sarcastically.

"And the Wiggles, I hope," said Brooke, clasping both hands to her chest in mock excitement.

"Idiots," said Olivia, tossing her head in disgust.

When Caitlin got home, her mother was on the phone. "Seven and a half years . . . as an occupational therapist," she was saying, "but anything really. Pardon? Yes, I am able to travel."

Caitlin got a couple of slices of frozen bread out of the freezer and put them in the microwave. She scanned the fridge for some juice but there wasn't any so she got some water and sat drumming her fingers on the kitchen bench. The microwave beeped loudly. Her mother frowned at her and waved her hand.

"Sorry," she said to the person on the other end of the phone. "I missed that."

When her mother finally finished, Caitlin grabbed the phone and headed upstairs.

"Hello to you too," her mother said to her retreating back.

The phone in the newsroom was answered by a grumpy male voice. "Megan? Yeah, hold on."

Megan came on the line, sounding a bit frazzled. "Hiya," she said. "Hey, I'm just up against it at the moment. I'll have to call you back."

"Okay," said Caitlin.

"I've sent an email. Have a look at—"

"Right," said Caitlin. She went downstairs but now her mother was on the computer.

"Arrrgh!" Caitlin grumbled. "I need that."

Her mother's fingers froze on the keyboard and her shoulders stiffened. "I'm writing a job application if you don't mind," she said, in a chilly voice. "I'm sorry if that's inconvenient, but you might find it even more inconvenient not having a house to live in."

"Jeez," muttered Caitlin, exiting the kitchen. "Someone needs a chill pill."

"What did you say?" called her mother but Caitlin was already halfway up the stairs. Back in her bedroom she lay on the floor, listening to music and teasing Skoota with a peacock feather. Finally, the phone rang.

"Sorry I couldn't talk to you before," said Megan breathlessly. "So, what do you reckon?"

"I haven't read your message," said Caitlin. "Mum's on the computer."

"Aw, okay," said Megan, sounding disappointed. "Hey, what was the name of that bike your mother had?"

"Ah . . . a Trail something. A Trail—"

"Blitza? A Trailblitza?"

"I think so," said Caitlin.

"Well, the thing is, there's this journo who's just started here. He used to work as a researcher on *Scam Busters*, you know that TV show on Channel 7?"

"Yeah."

"Anyway, I asked him if they ever had any complaints about dodgy bikes."

"Mmm."

"Well, he says he can remember one last year – about a bike called a Trailblitza. Anyway, that's what he thought it was. He can't remember all the details but thought there was some problem with the handlebars."

"Really?" said Caitlin. "Why didn't they do something?"

"They thought it was just a one-off."

"Does he still have the person's name, the one who complained?"

"No. That's the pain. Because they didn't think there was a story, he binned the notes."

"Bummer."

"Yeah, I know, but still . . ."

"Did you tell him about Mum?"

'Course not. I didn't think you'd want me to."

"No."

"This is your story. I reckon you're on to something, girl."

CHAPTER TWENTY-TWO

"Here, go and put these on the gate," said Rita, thrusting a bunch of pink and white balloons at Caitlin.

"Ah, I don't think so," said Caitlin, stepping back and holding up her palms. "I'm not turning five!"

"Oh dear, I think we've definitely got a teenager on our hands," groaned Granddad, taking the balloons. "Here, I'll put them out."

Caitlin scowled but thought better of arguing. She went to check herself in the hall mirror for about the twentieth time. She was wearing her new jeans – her mother's present to her – and a turquoise and white striped top that they'd bought from a mail order catalogue. Caitlin fluffed her hair, inspected her braces for any trapped food – not a good look – and stabbed concealer on a fresh pimple on her chin as the doorbell rang.

"You look so cooool," enthused Brooke, tripping

over the doorstep and practically landing in Caitlin's arms. "Happy Birthday!" They locked together in a fumbly embrace.

"Thank you," said Caitlin, blushing and re-fluffing her hair.

Olivia came through the door, wrestling with a sleeping bag and pillow and a red and yellow heart-shaped balloon. "Cool jeans," she said, standing back to look at Caitlin. "Let's see?"

Caitlin did a self-conscious twirl. "I had to get them taken up," she said. "They were like . . ." She stretched her arms in an exaggerated gesture.

"Can you see your crack when you sit down?" asked Brooke. Olivia snorted.

"No," said Caitlin.

"Cool," said Brooke, "I hate bum cracks on show."

Granddad was standing in the background, shaking his head. "What about your other present?" he said. "The one you can't wear." "Oh, yeah, yeah," said Caitlin jiggling excitedly. "I got a digital camera . . . from Granddad."

"Cool," said Olivia, with an anguished sigh. "You're sooo—"

"Yeah," said Caitlin, jogging towards the stairs. "Come on."

During the next half hour the doorbell rang repeatedly and the guests were sent up to join the squealing, chattering mob in Caitlin's room. Three hours later, pizza boxes containing little mounds of discarded toppings littered the lounge and Caitlin was putting on the second DVD, when her mother appeared in the doorway. "Excuse me," she yelled over the din.

"Were you expecting a boy?"

An electric shock seemed to blitz the room. Everybody's eyes swivelled to the door. "A boy?" said Caitlin.

"Yes," said Rita, reversing out. "There's one at the door." The girls leapt to their feet and followed Caitlin into the hallway.

Standing on the doorstep looking totally freaked by the mob descending on him, was Liam Marsden.

"Hi," said Caitlin, blushing furiously.

"Hi," said Liam, looking panic-stricken. "I . . . um . . . came to look at the printer."

Someone poked Caitlin in the back and she could hear stifled giggles behind her. She turned around and glowered at her friends. "Right," said Caitlin. "Do you want to come in. . .?"

Liam thrust his hands deep in his pockets forcing his baggy jeans further down on his hips. "No way . . . I mean . . . uh . . . I can come back another time . . . I didn't know . . ."

"Sorry," said Caitlin. "If that's okay."

With a relieved look Liam scurried off.

"Byeeeeee, Liam," chorused the partygoers as he bolted down the path.

THE NEXT MORNING, as Brooke and Olivia slept, Caitlin hauled herself out of bed. Her limbs felt heavy, her head fuzzy and she had a dull ache in her stomach, probably from eating too much pizza and chocolate the night before. She grumpily stepped over Brooke and Olivia wrapped in their warm cocoons, and grabbed her robe from the back of the door.

Downstairs, she fed Skoota, fixed breakfast, unloaded the dishwasher and put some washing out. An hour and a half later she went back up to her bedroom. Brooke was just waking. She hauled herself up onto her elbows, her dark hair falling across her face.

"Where have you been?" she croaked. Olivia groaned and wriggled further into her cocoon.

"There's some breakfast downstairs," said Caitlin, sweeping the curtains open, then under her breath, "though it's practically lunchtime."

~

AT SCHOOL ON MONDAY, Caitlin went looking for Liam. She found him with a group of friends, sitting on the grass near the hall. He got up and came over.

"Hiya," said Caitlin.

"Hi," said Liam, glancing back at his mates, who were pulling faces and shouting comments they couldn't quite hear.

"Thanks for coming on Saturday," said Caitlin. "Sorry I was . . . busy."

Liam shrugged. "Sweet. No worries." He shuffled and cast another glance towards his noisy mates. "Okay then," he said, and started to head off.

"Can you still look at our printer?" asked Caitlin.

"Sure," said Liam, "when?" An apple core sailed through the air and hit him on the arm. He frowned at his friends and lowered his voice. "I probably can't come till the weekend."

"Right," said Caitlin. "That's cool. Thanks."

~

On Saturday afternoon, Caitlin was pegging out a load of washing, when Liam materialised from behind a bed sheet.

"Ohmigod!" she said.

"Sorry," he said. "I thought you'd seen me."

"No . . . I didn't," she said breathlessly.

Caitlin invited Liam inside and introduced him to her mother, who was in the living room combing through the jobs section of the paper.

"Hello Liam," she said. "I hear you're a bit of a computer whiz."

"Not really," said Liam. Caitlin noticed his shyness with her mother and the way his fringe fell like a curtain over his eyes as he tilted his head.

"C'mon," said Caitlin. "I'll show you where it is."

Liam looked at the printer and frowned. "I see what you mean. It is pretty . . . retro."

"Huh!' said Caitlin, punching him on the arm.

"Sorry," he said "but it is. You could replace this for about two hundred and fifty bucks."

"Go an' tell that to my mum," said Caitlin, "and get your head bitten off. That's practically her entire benefit for the week."

While Liam clicked away expertly on the computer, Caitlin sat beside him sipping a ginger beer. It seemed totally natural. Away from school and the taunts of her mates, her nervousness around him evaporated.

"Ahh . . ." Liam said suddenly.

"What?" said Caitlin peering at the screen.

"You've deleted the printer."

"Deleted it?"

"Yeah, somehow you've deleted the connection. That's why it's not working." He clicked the mouse a couple of times. "There, it's back."

"Must've been Mum," said Caitlin. "She's hopeless with computers."

"No, it was you," said Liam.

"Really?" said Caitlin, astonished. "How do you know?"

"It had your electronic fingerprint on it."

"True?" said Caitlin, wide-eyed.

"Yep," said Liam, grinning.

Caitlin inspected his face and smiled. "Liar," she said and elbowed him in the ribs.

After he'd fixed the printer, Liam downloaded a free virus protection update and did some other things that made the computer go faster. "Mum'll be stoked," said Caitlin. "She's been job searching and she's always complaining about how slow it is."

"Job searching," said Liam, flicking the top off his ginger beer. "How come she needs a job?"

"Because she's bored," said Caitlin.

"True?"

"No . . . well yes, but mostly we need the money," said Caitlin, shrugging.

Liam frowned. "But if that bike was dodgy like you say, why don't you just sue the idiot that sold it to you?" Caitlin gazed at Liam with growing respect.

CHAPTER TWENTY-THREE

Caitlin checked her mum wasn't anywhere within earshot and picked up the phone. A recorded voice said, "You have reached the Ministry of Consumer Affairs," then gave a range of numbers you could dial to get the right department. Caitlin frowned and pressed 2. "Complaints, can I help you," said a bored-sounding woman.

"I, ah, want to report a dangerous product," said Caitlin nervously.

"Right," said the woman. "I can send you out some forms or you can do it online."

"Oh, okay," said Caitlin. "It's a bike. My mum—"

Just put all the details in your complaint," said the woman briskly. "Do you want me to send you the forms?"

"Yes, that would be—"

"Online's quicker."

"Right," said Caitlin.

"So what do you want to do?"

"Um . . . online . . . I'll do it online."

"Okay," said the woman. "Just go to our website and follow the instructions."

"Right," said Caitlin. "I'll—"

"Anything else I can help with?"

"No . . . I . . . "

"Thank you." *Click.*

Caitlin was relieved to find her mum wasn't on the computer but as she walked into the family room she couldn't help noticing a basket of washing waiting to be folded and the lunch dishes piled in the sink. Granddad usually helped over the weekend but he was in bed with the flu.

With a heavy sigh, Caitlin plonked herself in front of the computer and went to the Consumer Affairs website. She clicked her way through the Product Safety section and came across a reference to bikes: *'All pedal bicycles sold must comply with safety standards. A trader can be fined for selling a bike that does not meet the required standard for bicycles and that is proved to be unsafe.'*

"Fined?" said Caitlin. She clicked on another heading, Reporting Unsafe Products. It said: *'The Ministry of Consumer Affairs encourages consumers to report unsafe products. If we don't know about it, we cannot do anything about it.'*

"Exactly," she said, flexing her fingers.

It took her about half an hour to complete the safety incident form and fire it off. Feeling pleased with herself, she switched off the computer and turned her attention to searching the diminishing contents of the freezer for something for dinner.

~

NEXT DAY, during maths, a runner came into the classroom, and handed a note to Mrs Bowman. The teacher took off her reading glasses and scanned the room. "Caitlin," she said. "You're wanted at the office."

Caitlin gathered up her things and quickly headed over to the admin block. Mrs Crystal, the principal's secretary, greeted her at the door. "Ah, Caitlin," she said. "Don't want to worry you dear, but you're needed at home."

Caitlin immediately began to worry.

"A Mr" – she looked down at a piece of paper in her hand – "Philip Dalgety is coming to collect you."

Phil? Caitlin's mind went into overdrive. It had to be her mum. Something had happened to her mum. She sat on the chair outside Mrs Crystal's office, her eyes fixed on the school driveway, her foot bobbing flat out. A few minutes later Phil's 4WD cruised to a halt outside the door.

"It's your granddad," Phil explained. "He's been taken to hospital."

On the way to the hospital, Caitlin fired questions at Phil but it seemed there were very few he could answer. He said he'd had a call from her mum to say that Granddad had been rushed to hospital. "She asked me to get you from school and take you there. I don't know any more than that."

~

CAITLIN CRIED SILENTLY as she looked down on her Granddad. He was propped up on starched white pillows, an oxygen mask over his nose and mouth and a drip in his arm. His skin looked almost as grey as his wavy hair and his chest rose and fell in quick gasps. She looked up at her mother, sitting on the other side of the bed, stroking Granddad's hand.

"Is he going to die?" she asked in a quivery voice.

Her mother smiled. "No, love. 'Course he's not."

"But he looks terrible." "He's pretty sick." "What's wrong with him."

"Pneumonia."

"Pneumonia?" gasped Caitlin, "but that's really bad."

"It's not good, but there are powerful drugs to fight it these days."

"How did he get it?"

"The doctor says it's a complication of the flu."

"Poor Granddad." Caitlin lifted his hand and gently placed it in hers. She winced at the needle disappearing under a sticky bandage. Apart from the usual colds, she'd never known Granddad to be sick, and she'd certainly never seen him in pyjamas with a stubbly chin and his wavy hair all fluffy.

"You must be hungry," said Mum. "Let's go down to the cafeteria."

Caitlin frowned. "What about—?"

"He needs to rest," said Mum. "We won't be long."

Caitlin reluctantly left her grandfather and wheeled her mother through the wide hospital corridors. Bright fluorescent lights reflected off the shiny linoleum floor and a cocktail of hospital smells – disinfectant, boiled vegetables and sickness – filled their nostrils.

As they moved down the corridor, they passed a succession of rooms, glimpsing a woman in a chair by the window, her pretzel-thin legs sticking from her pale blue nightgown, two children playing a board game with a white-haired man, and two nurses making a bed, a stiff sheet billowing in the air for a moment before coming to rest on a plastic-coated mattress.

Caitlin and her mum stayed at the hospital until 10pm. when Phil came to take them home. While Caitlin trudged wearily up the stairs to bed, Phil stayed for coffee and Caitlin drifted to sleep to the quiet buzz of voices downstairs.

~

With Granddad laid up, Caitlin busied herself trying to keep the household running. Phil took over the supermarket shopping and organised for someone to mow the lawn but there was still heaps to do. He also took Caitlin to hockey practice on Wednesday and, instead of standing on the sideline, he helped with ball drills and made up the numbers in a mock game. On the way home he was full of advice. "That was a great goal you scored," he said. "Pity it was for the other team!"

"I couldn't help it," protested Caitlin. "It just bounced off my stick."

Phil gave her a sideways glance and put on an exaggerated girly voice. "I couldn't help it. It just bounced off my stick."

Caitlin laughed. "Well, it did."

"It was the way you were holding your stick, you nong."

"Huh?"

"Your stick was leaning backwards. It acts as ramp for the ball to roll up. Wonder you didn't smash your teeth. You should always hold it slanting away from you."

"Whatever."

"No, you should – always. Can't believe you've played hockey this long without having that drilled into you."

Caitlin pulled a face and began jiggling and swaying to a song on the car radio. She turned it up. "I love this," she said, beginning to sing along. Phil just smiled and shook his head.

On Monday Caitlin came home from school to an empty house. Her mum was at the hospital. She found a letter from the Ministry of Consumer Affairs sitting on the bench.

She tore it open and read: *Thank you for your incident report regarding the Trailblitza Mountain Bike. The Ministry takes the issue of bicycle safety seriously and any breaches of compulsory safety standards, where proven, are urgently acted on. However, as this is the first and only complaint we have had about this particular product, we have decided not to proceed with an investigation at this stage. All complaints are entered in a database and where there is a pattern the Ministry will take some action.*

Caitlin threw the letter down in disgust and turned to the pantry for comfort. After she'd constructed and disposed of a huge peanut butter and honey sandwich, she picked up the phone and dialled the number on the top of the letter. She drummed her fingers impatiently as the recorded message trundled through. Finally, she got through to someone she could actually have a conversation with.

"It's Caitlin Nove," she explained. "I wrote to you about my mum's bike accident."

"Yes."

"She's in a wheelchair."

"I'm sorry."

"Well, the thing is . . . she's not the only one."

"Right."

"There's this musician – Peter Lee – and someone else complained to a TV show."

"Right, just a moment dear . . ." Caitlin could hear a muffled conversation.

The lady came back on the line.

"How old are you, dear?"

Caitlin was silent. She could feel heat rising in her chest. "Thirteen," she said.

"Pardon?"

Caitlin cleared her throat. "I'm thirteen."

There was a pause.

"Is this for a school project?"

"No. My mother had an accident. On a bike. The handlebars snapped off. "

"Right," said the woman. "Having something like this happen to your mum is a terrible thing."

"It's not about—"

"How is she, by the way?" Caitlin gripped the phone tightly and fumed. How dare this woman who'd never even met her mother pretend to be so concerned. "Are you there?"

"Yes," said Caitlin, through clenched teeth. "The bike was dangerous . . . and there are more out there."

"Right. Well . . . thank you for your call, Carolyn."

"Caitlin."

"Sorry, Caitlin. We'll be sure to keep your complaint and if we get any others . . ."

"But I have. There are—"

"Well, you'll need to fill in another incident form. We'll need brand names and serial numbers."

"Right," said Caitlin. "I guess—"

"Thank you for your call." Click.

"Errrrrggggh," said Caitlin, stabbing the disconnect button.

CHAPTER TWENTY-FOUR

Caitlin marched into the hospital bursting with things to tell her granddad. She'd caught the bus through town after school and felt extremely proud of herself, not only for that, but also for negotiating the maze of corridors to find the right ward. She bustled into the room, her first sentence forming on her lips, only to find Granddad's bed empty. The bedclothes were pulled back and she could still see the indent of his body on the crumpled bottom sheet.

Her heart flipped. She imagined him flat out in the emergency room, big paddles being applied to his chest like in those TV hospital dramas. "Stand back!" ZAP! Her legs felt shaky and she sank into a chair beside the bed

"He's gone to X-ray," said a deep voice from the bed opposite. Caitlin looked over to see a big man, bald, with a large nose and a wide smile.

Caitlin smiled shyly back. "Oh, okay," she said, clasping her hands between her knees.

"I'm sure he won't be long."

"Thanks," said Caitlin. She sank further into the chair and felt her heartbeat start to slow. As she waited, she scanned the array of Granddad's things on the bedside cabinet. There was a small radio, with earplugs, a half-finished crossword on a page folded from a newspaper, a pair of black-framed reading glasses, a speckled banana, a mandarin, an unopened packet of chocolate-coated almonds, and a plastic jug of orange cordial. Propped on the windowsill were an array of get well cards, a vase of yellow and purple chrysanthemums and a fancy posy from a florist's shop, with its own spongy watering system.

Caitlin wondered if it would be cheeky to open the almonds. She'd come straight from school and was feeling really hungry. She was pondering this when someone spoke, causing her to jump. The voice said: "You're Caitlin, right?" It was the bald man again.

She smiled, "Yes," she said, "I am."

"I've heard a lot about you," he said.

Caitlin blushed and gave a little laugh.

"Your granddad never stops talking about you."

Caitlin nodded an awkward smile and looked at the floor. Just then, voices in the corridor drew her eyes to the door. An orderly and a nurse came in wheeling a slim bed. On board, nestled in two plump, arctic-white pillows, was her granddad, looking tired and pale, an oxygen tube in his nose.

"Hello pet," he said, lifting a sluggish hand.

"Hi Granddad," said Caitlin, leaning over and attempting a hug.

"He'll be all yours, soon as we get him back into bed," said the nurse.

Caitlin stood back while the orderly and nurse expertly transferred Granddad from the trolley to the bed. The nurse, her long dark plait bobbing as she adjusted the back of the bed, checked the drip, scrawled something on a clipboard, and washed her hands at a nearby basin.

"Feel like something to eat, Mr Nove?" she asked, blotting her hands with a paper towel.

Caitlin watched Granddad shake his head.

"Tea then?"

Granddad nodded.

"Okay, I'll chase some up," she said and padded briskly out of the room.

Caitlin pulled the chair closer to the bed. "You should have something to eat, Granddad," she said, looking concerned.

"I had some porridge this morning," he said, in a weary voice. "At least that's what they said it was." He gave a short chuckle and Caitlin caught a momentary glimpse of the old granddad but the effort seemed to tire him. He reached out and took Caitlin's hand. His skin felt warm and rough. "So, what've you been up to?"

"Well . . ." Caitlin talked nonstop for about ten minutes. She told him about hockey – how they'd won on Saturday, and about how Phil was too noisy on the sidelines and she was considering banning him. She told him how her mum was learning to drive the car with hand controls, and how Skoota had sicked up a fur ball into Caitlin's schoolbag and she'd only realised when she reached in for her pencil case.

Granddad laughed but it made him cough so Caitlin tried not to tell him anything else that was too funny. "Oh, and Mum said to tell you that Mrs Lusk is watering your garden and collecting your mail. She's got Buddie at her place and she's stuffing your freezer with casseroles."

"That's nice," said Granddad, relaxing into his pillows. A food trolley rattled down the corridor accompanied by a burst of chatter from two orderlies. Caitlin plucked a limp chrysanthemum out of the vase on the windowsill.

"How is your mum?" asked Granddad.

"Good," said Caitlin. "Phil's taking her to see about that job today."

"Hmm," said Granddad.

"I think it will be good for her. She's bored as. Needs to get a life."

Granddad shook his head. "Some life," he said. His voice trailed off.

Caitlin looked at him. His eyes were glistening and his hands were clutching at the covers. "Granddad," she whispered, the smile fading from her face.

"She deserved better," he said, his lips quivering.

"Granddad, c'mon . . ." Caitlin reached out and patted his hand, weathered and tanned against the white sheets.

"I really messed it up for her . . ."

"You didn't," said Caitlin, smiling nervously. "You—"

". . . and for you too." Caitlin's stomach clenched.

"No, hey, c'mon Granddad."

The old man shook his head and his face crumpled. He looked deep into Caitlin's eyes. "Your father . . ."

Caitlin swallowed and squeezed his hand. "Granddad, I know," she said. "I know."

His eyes locked with hers for a moment longer, as bewilderment turned to relief. Caitlin watched him take a deep breath. His warm, rough hand closed around hers. "You were the best thing to happen to her," he said, "and me. I just couldn't see it back then." His chest shuddered and he squeezed his eyes shut.

Caitlin grabbed a tissue from a box on the bedside cabinet and pressed it into his hand. "You'll be right soon, Granddad." She squeezed his hand.

"Look at me," he said with a quivery smile. "Hopeless. I just don't want to add to her troubles, love. I couldn't bear to . . ."

Caitlin swallowed. "Don't be silly." There was an awkward silence.

"What do you have to do to get a bedpan around here!" someone yelled from the room next door.

Caitlin couldn't help herself. She burst out laughing. Granddad started laughing too, and began to cough. When he recovered, much to Caitlin's relief, he was still smiling. "Take no notice of me, love," he said, waving his hand dismissively. "Feeling a bit sorry for myself, aren't I?"

"Ah, just a bit," said Caitlin. She pulled the blanket up over his chest and folded it back. "What you need is a good sleep," she said, "and I'd better go, got heaps of homework."

Granddad nodded. "Thanks for coming, pet," he said, his heavy hand hovering just above the bedclothes. "Take those chocolate nuts. I can't stand them."

Caitlin's eyes lit up. "Are you sure?"

"Yes," he said in a raspy whisper. "But don't tell Mrs Lusk. I think she sent them."

"Sweet," said Caitlin, slipping the box into her back pack. She kissed Granddad on the cheek and he smiled drowsily.

"You're a good girl," he whispered. By the time she reached the door, he was snoring gently.

~

THE REST of Caitlin's week disappeared in a blur of chores, homework and visits to the hospital. On Sunday, just after she and her mum got back, there was a knock on the door. Caitlin opened it to find Liam standing there, a printer in his arms. "My dad's got a new one," he said, before she could protest.

Rita said they couldn't possibly accept the printer and couldn't they buy it rather than take it? She finally insisted on ringing Liam's father to thank him. As she gushed on and on, Caitlin rolled her eyes and took Liam into the family room where he began installing the new printer.

Caitlin watched him thoughtfully, her mind working overtime, as usual. "You know what you said about suing that guy?"

"Huh?" said Liam.

"You know, the guy who sold the bike that Mum—"

"Oh, yeah," said Liam, heaving the old printer off the cabinet and, to Caitlin's embarrassment, uncovering a thick layer of dust, three bobby pins, a lip balm and six dead flies.

"Ooh, gross," she said, disappearing and coming back with a tea towel. Liam pretended to cough and splutter as she flicked at the dusty surface.

"There," she said, flinging the tea towel in the corner. "Anyway, that guy . . ."

"Yeah?" said Liam, pulling out wires and plugging others in.

"Do you think we could sue him?"

"Huh. That's a bit odd," said Liam distractedly, inspecting a tangle of cords on the floor.

"Oh, I see." Caitlin waited patiently until he'd finished.

"Okay, that should work," he said, lowering himself on to the swivel chair. "What were you saying?"

"That guy who sold the bike. I know of two other people the same thing happened to."

"What thing?"

"The handlebars snapping off."

"True? Were they hurt?"

"One was. Don't know about the other." Liam looked impressed.

"That's criminal."

"Do you really think we could sue him?"

"Dunno," shrugged Liam. "Who is he?"

"That's the problem," frowned Caitlin. "We don't know."

"Shouldn't be hard to find out," said Liam, his hands poised over the keyboard. "What was the company called?" Liam googled 'International Importers' but kept coming up with the same Asian Food company Phil had tracked down. "Okay," he said, pushing up his sleeves. "When did you buy the bike?"

"Christmas, last year," said Caitlin. "It was in a flyer in the letterbox."

Liam tried 'cheap bikes', 'Xmas bikes' and a number of other combinations but nothing of interest came up. "Okay. Where'd you get it?" he asked.

"It was a shop in the Grenville Shopping Centre. You know that place. It's been empty for ages."

Liam thought for a moment. "Oh yeah, used to be that bargain basement place. Toys and stuff."

"Yeah," said Caitlin. "But the bikes looked quite good."

"Yeah right!" said Liam, rolling his eyes.

"Well, anyway," said Caitlin, defensively, "they should have been safe."

"Totally," said Liam. He looked thoughtful for a moment, then said, "Hey, I think my sister's friend worked there."

"Where?"

"That place that sold the bikes. Cassie. Yeah, I'm sure she did. In the Christmas holidays."

"Really?" said Caitlin, her eyes widening. "Yeah, she'll know the guy," said Liam, his thumb already punching out a text.

~

After a week in hospital, Granddad was discharged but Caitlin's mum insisted he come and stay with them. He put up quite a fight but Caitlin noticed her mother was surprisingly insistent and, in his weakened state, Granddad had no choice but to agree. "But just till I'm on my feet again," he grumbled.

Caitlin quite enjoyed coming home after school to find Granddad sitting in the front room reading or doing a crossword. After dinner they played Scrabble or cards or watched TV. Often Caitlin had to rescue a cup of tea and remove Granddad's glasses as he drifted to sleep in the chair.

One day, as she was cycling to school, late as usual, Caitlin felt her phone vibrate in her pocket. She stopped and checked it. It was a text from Liam.

Got news. C U @ intvl.

Cool, Caitlin replied and pedalled furiously to avoid another detention.

~

WHEN SHE LEFT her friends at interval to go and meet Liam, there were the usual jibes.

"It must be luurrve," said Olivia, looking coy and twirling her fringe.

"Gotta be," said Brooke, arching her dark brows.

"Grow up," said Caitlin and she strode purposefully over to the sports field where Liam and his mates hung out.

Caitlin could see Liam and two other boys kicking a ball around. Liam was laughing as he twisted and turned his body, skilfully blocking another boy's attempts to get the ball. His school socks had fallen around his ankles, his legs were flecked with mud and his face flushed from the effort. He finally glanced over and acknowledged Caitlin with a flick of his eyebrows, but made no move to come over.

Caitlin folded her arms and waited. She felt like everyone was gawping at her.

By the time Liam scooped up his jersey and sauntered over, she was furious. "Take your time, why don't you," she said, when he finally rocked up.

"Whoa!" said Liam, reeling back. "What's up with you?"

"Nothing," said Caitlin, testily. "What do you want?" She didn't mean to sound so sharp but she was angry and she just wanted out of there.

"I don't think I'll tell you now," said Liam.

"Oh, whatever," said Caitlin. She turned around and stomped off, her fists balled, and her face burning. A group of girls sniggered as she passed.

Back in class Olivia asked, unwisely, "How was Liam?"

"Fine," said Caitlin, slapping her workbook on the desk. "What page did she say?"

CHAPTER TWENTY-FIVE

Caitlin stomped in the door that afternoon to a familiar aroma wafting from the kitchen. Her ragged day was forgotten for a moment as she followed her nose to the kitchen. There she found Granddad easing a tray of scones from the oven.

"Sweet," said Caitlin, dumping her bag in the middle of the floor and advancing on him.

"Whoa, get off!" he protested, waving a tattered oven glove at her. "They're hot, hot, hot!"

Caitlin collapsed onto a stool. "But I'm starving"

"Good," said Granddad, sliding the tray onto the top of the oven. "They won't go to waste then, will they?"

Caitlin noticed his movements were slow and there was a weariness to his voice. She felt a twinge of guilt. "You're not supposed to be doing stuff," she said.

"It's just a batch of scones." She watched

Granddad hang the oven glove back on a brass hook near the stove. "Hot chocolate?"

"Yes . . . I can get it."

"It's all right."

"Granddad," said Caitlin, sliding off the stool and pointing at it. "Sit down." Granddad opened his mouth to protest then shut it again and shuffled over to the stool. With a little grunt, he eased himself on to it.

"Good. Now . . . tea, coffee or hot chocolate?"

"Whatever," said Granddad. "Tea, I guess."

Caitlin raised her eyebrows.

"Yes, tea then. Thanks."

"Granddad," said Caitlin, as she filled the jug. "What did you do with Mum's bike?"

"Why?" He eyeballed her suspiciously.

"I just wondered," said Caitlin.

"I dumped it," said Granddad.

"You didn't!" said Caitlin, a little too loud.

"Why would I want to keep it?" he said. "I feel bad enough about buying the blasted thing."

"It wasn't your fault it was dodgy," said Caitlin.

"Oh don't start that again. You don't know it was 'dodgy'."

"Actually, I do," said Caitlin. She put the lid on the teapot and turned to Granddad. "And I am not letting it drop, so there." She poked her tongue cheekily and braced herself for the reaction – but it never came.

Instead, Granddad looked at her intently. "As if I

could stop you," he said. "Just mind how you go." Caitlin smiled. "I mean it," he warned. "Now, is that tea coming any time soon?"

CAITLIN STARED out her bedroom window. The sky was dark and rain was beginning to fall. She sat heavily on her bed, disturbing Skoota, who looked irritated and curled himself into a tighter ball. Caitlin smiled and looked up. Her eyes locked with the cool gaze of Aunt Viola staring from the frame on her bedside cabinet. She picked up her phone and started to text Liam but changed her mind and tossed it aside.

Biting her lip she scratched Skoota under the chin. She must have touched the tender spot where the abscess was still healing because he responded with a swift bite. Caitlin watched as blood oozed from two punctures on the back of her hand.

On Saturday, Phil turned up to take Caitlin to hockey and as they travelled to the game, he was full of advice. "Now, remember to pass it out to the wing today, that's what Natalie's there for."

Caitlin rolled her eyes. "Yes."

"And remember to keep your stick down. I see all you girls with your sticks waving in the air like golf clubs. Can't trap a ball like that." Caitlin groaned and rolled her eyes. "Since when did you become an expert on hockey?"

"Since I was appointed team taxi and assistant coach."

"Whatever," said Caitlin, reclining the seat and closing her eyes.

On their way back from hockey, Phil called into Granddad's. The rubbish bin needed to be put out and Mrs Lusk had called to say she had some baking to be collected.

Phil hoisted up the garage door and was hauling the wheelie bin noisily down the driveway when Mrs Lusk appeared at the fence. Caitlin watched as she handed over two plastic containers. As Phil settled in for a chat, Caitlin decided to check the garage to see if Granddad really had dumped the bike. She suspected he'd just said that to get her to give up the investigation. She walked into the garage and scanned every inch but the bike had definitely gone.

"What's up?" asked Phil, when he returned to find Caitlin standing, arms folded, in the middle of the garage.

"The bike," she said. "It's gone."

"Probably a good thing," said Phil, easing the top off one of the plastic containers and helping himself to a muffin.

Caitlin frowned. "It was evidence," she said testily.

"Oh, right," said Phil, munching, "I didn't know you were still—"

"Well I am," said Caitlin, "and they need the serial number."

"Who?"

"The people at Consumer Affairs. They need serial numbers to investigate."

"Oh, right. Sorry – did you want one?" He held out the container. She shook her head.

After Phil had scoffed down a couple of muffins, he got the stepladder and checked the rafters. "Nothing up here," he reported to Caitlin, his voice almost lost in the ceiling cavity. "Seems he's definitely dumped it."

"Yeah," said Caitlin glumly. "That's Granddad all right – out of sight, out of mind."

CHAPTER TWENTY-SIX

"Damn. What can we do?" pondered Megan when Caitlin phoned her that evening. "Are you absolutely sure it's gone?"

"Absolutely."

"Right," said Megan. Caitlin could almost hear her brain ticking. "I could ask Peter Lee if his friend's still got his."

"He won't have," said Caitlin glumly.

"Worth a try," said Megan. "I'll call you back."

A short time later the phone rang. "Bad news," reported Megan. "The only bit of the bike Peter's friend has is the bit he brought to the restaurant."

"Right," said Caitlin.

"I think we're stuffed," said Megan.

"Yeah," said Caitlin gloomily, "and that crook will get away with it."

"Hopefully not," said Megan. "Let's not give up just yet."

THE MONTHLY SCHOOL council meeting finally thrust Liam and Caitlin together but he barely acknowledged her as he walked into the room and sat at the other end of the table. It was a short meeting, devoted mostly to discussing a proposal for resurfacing the hockey turf.

After the meeting, Caitlin jogged to catch up with Liam but he kept striding along, responding to her questions with sulky grunts. She knew that any information he had wouldn't be much use to her now but she didn't like the big freeze between them and had to admit that maybe she'd overreacted, just a tiny bit.

"Look, I'm sorry about the other day," she blurted, finally catching up to him. "I just . . . you just left me standing there."

"And that's a crime?"

"Yes . . . I mean, no . . . I felt stupid."

"Not as stupid as you looked, yelling and stomping off like a total fruit loop." Liam gave her a hurtful sideways glance.

"Well, I'm sorry."

"Whatever."

"What did you want anyway?" asked Caitlin.

Liam looked sulky. "Why should I tell you?"

"Liam, please."

Liam stopped walking, frowned and thrust his hands in his pockets.

"Oh c'mon," pleaded Caitlin. "I've said sorry."

He continued looking down and scuffing his shoe on the concrete.

"Okay," said Caitlin, starting to walk off. "See you round."

"Hold on," said Liam. He sighed and slowly pulled something out of his pocket. He thrust a scrap of paper at Caitlin. There was a name on it.

"Connor Sampson," she read. She looked at Liam, puzzled. "Who's he?"

"The dude that ran the bike shop," he said casually.

Caitlin looked at the name again and felt a ripple of excitement as she repeated it, "Connor Sampson." She looked up at Liam. "Thanks," she said. "I owe you."

Liam shrugged. "What are you going to do now?"

Caitlin folded the paper and put it in her pocket. "Don't know. Granddad's dumped the bike, unfortunately. Guess there's not much I can do."

"Why not?"

"Well, we haven't got any evidence."

Liam bounced on the balls of his feet, an odd smirk on his face. "Ah, but maybe we have," he said

"What are you talking about?" asked Caitlin, annoyed at having to extract every last detail.

"He's got a stack of bikes in his garage."

Caitlin blinked. "Who?"

"He lives on Tolley Drive," said Liam. "You know, over near the river. His number's unlisted but

Mrs Weavers helped me track down his address through the electoral roll."

Caitlin realized she was standing with her mouth open. She snapped it shut.

Liam smiled. "Thought you'd be interested."

"But how do you know . . .?"

"About the bikes? I looked through his garage window."

"You went there?" asked Caitlin.

Liam nodded. "Not sure if they're the same as your mum's but there are heaps of them."

Caitlin could hardly contain her excitement. Her mind was working overtime. "We should so go there – and maybe take some photos," she said.

"Yeah, yeah, we could," said Liam. "Have to make sure no one's there first."

"Course," said Caitlin. "I'm not stu—"

"Okay," said Liam. "I was just saying. How about Saturday?" he suggested.

Caitlin thought for a moment. She'd organised to go to the zoo with Mum and her friends but she wasn't going to tell Liam that. "No, I can't do Saturday," she said.

"Right. How about Sunday?"

"Sunday's cool," said Caitlin. "See you then."

CHAPTER TWENTY-SEVEN

The baboons regarded the group with lazy disdain. A big male – deliberately it seemed - turned his bottom to them.

"Oh yuck," Caitlin spluttered, waving her hands in front of her like an out-of-control helicopter.

"Gross," said Olivia, wincing at the puffy crimson backside on display. Then the baboon began inspecting his crotch.

"Eewww," said Caitlin, collapsing onto Brooke's shoulder.

"He looks like Mr Gifkins," observed Olivia drily.

"He does. He does," shrieked Caitlin, giggling and jiggling as though she might wet her pants. A gaggle of Japanese tourists shuffled quickly away.

"And that one looks like Mrs Critchly," pointed Olivia.

"Which one?" asked Caitlin.

"The one with the titties," whispered Olivia. Caitlin and Brooke shrieked and clung to each other like drunken sailors. The baboons became unsettled and a man in tartan pants, clutching a camera, frowned at the girls.

"Calm down," said Rita. She was squinting at a map covered in little animal symbols and interconnecting pathways.

"I need food," said Caitlin, wiping her eyes.

"I don't think I could face lunch," said Brooke, applying some rose-coloured lip gloss.

"Can I have some?" asked Caitlin, holding out her hand.

"You guys'll get meningitis sharing that," said Olivia.

"Quite right," said Mum.

"Whatever," said Caitlin smacking her lips. "At least I'll look gorrr-jus on my deathbed. Hey, Mum, what about lunch?"

"Uh?"

"Food, mother. We need food."

"I was just . . . now, if the monkey enclosure is there and we're here . . ." Rita moved her finger around the map. "The band rotunda must be . . ."

"Over there," offered Brooke, "I think."

"Mum, you're such a ditz with maps," said Caitlin leaning over her mother. "Give it here."

"Don't snatch, Caitlin!"

Caitlin ignored her mother and studied the map.

"Hmm . . . let's see. Mum, you're a total ditzo. The band rotunda's back that way!"

"How?"

"I can never read those maps either," said Olivia, smiling.

Caitlin grabbed the handles of the wheelchair and whizzed her mum down the sloping path, as nervous parents shepherded toddlers out of the way and elderly folk, worried about their papery skin and brittle bones, hugged the handrail.

"Caitlin," said Mum, when they came to an abrupt stop. "If I need your help, I'll ask for it."

"Sorry," shrugged Caitlin, not looking sorry at all. "Let's have lunch under that tree." She eased her backpack off and unloaded a plastic container holding chicken sandwiches and banana cake wrapped in foil. From a bag on the back of the wheelchair, she took some plates, plastic tumblers and a large bottle of apple juice. Brooke and Olivia went to find the toilet.

"He said he'd meet us here at one o'clock," said Mum, looking at her watch.

"Who?" asked Caitlin, laying down a rug.

"Phil."

"Phil? You never told me he was coming."

"I did."

"I don't think so, Mum. I'd remember that."

"Well, he is."

"That's nice."

"What?"

"Nothing."

After they'd eaten, Caitlin lay on the grass, hitching up her T-shirt to get some sun on her stomach. "Imagine being an albino," she said, randomly.

"Huh?" said Olivia.

"An albino. It would be awful, eh?"

"S'pose."

"Yeah, like that girl in Year Eight," said Brooke. "She looks like a guinea pig with glasses."

"Sad. She can't help it."

"Better than being a bum-face baboon," said Caitlin. The others almost choked on their chicken sandwiches. Caitlin's mum frowned.

"I reckon if Mrs Pickford was an animal she'd be a fox," said Olivia. "Those beady little eyes . . ."

"Hey, yeah," said Caitlin, "and that pointy nose . . ."

"And that awful bushy ponytail," said Brooke. "Far out."

"Mrs Bowman would be an otter," said Caitlin.

"Why?" asked Brooke, cleaning her finger nails with a twig.

"Whiskers."

"Has she got whiskers?"

"Has she ever!" said Caitlin. "When she stands in the sun – you know, over by the window – there are all these bristles . . ."

"Gross," said Brooke. She looked thoughtful. "If I was an animal, I reckon I'd be an antelope." As if to demonstrate the anatomical similarities, she stretched out her long legs in front of her.

"I wonder where he is." Rita said, dropping her cellphone onto her lap.

"I'd like to be a cheetah," said Caitlin.

"So you could cheat in exams?" said Olivia.

Oh ha ha," said Caitlin. "No, so I could blitz everybody in the cross country."

"Yeah," said Olivia, "imagine Grace Carter's face . . ."

"Yeah."

"... when you went flying past."

"I'd probably chomp through her jugular on the way and still win."

"Well she'd be dead, wouldn't she, so of course you'd win."

"I'd be an elephant," said Olivia. The other two spluttered with laugher.

"Keep eating those school pies and you might just get your wish," said Caitlin.

"No, no. It would be so cool," insisted Olivia. "To be so big no one could hurt you."

"Aw, duh. What about elephant hunters?" said Brooke. Olivia scowled and reached for her drink.

"Here he is," said Rita, peering past the band rotunda and waving her arms. The girls watched as a tall figure in a green baseball cap came striding towards them.

"Move anything breakable," said Caitlin.

"That's mean," giggled Mum.

"Any tucker left?" said Phil, lowering himself onto the lawn. "Or have you gannets cleaned it all up?"

Caitlin noticed how Brooke and Olivia blushed and suddenly became less talkative.

"I'd given up on you," said Caitlin's mum. "Where did you get to?"

"Ended up doing a much bigger shop than I thought," said Phil, stylish as always in khaki cargo pants, a lemon sweatshirt and wrap-around sunglasses. "The supermarket was jam-packed. It was chaos."

"Thanks for doing that. Dad should be up to it again before too long."

"No problem," said Phil. He flicked the lid off a plastic container and helped himself to a sandwich.

"Hey, Mum, can we have an ice cream?" asked Caitlin, sitting up and smoothing down her T-shirt.

"You've just had lunch," said Phil.

"So?" said Caitlin cheekily. "Mum?"

Her mother sighed. "All right, pass me my purse."

"I'll get them," said Phil, reaching into his pocket.

"No, you won't," protested Mum.

"Yes, he will," said Caitlin, grabbing the ten-dollar note out of Phil's hand. "Thanks Phil." She skipped off with her friends, leaving her mother frowning and shaking her head.

The trio bought an ice cream each from the kiosk and sat on a bench nearby to eat it. "So, are your

Mum and Phil an item?" asked Olivia, peering through the trees to where the two of them were sitting.

"No, they're just friends really," said Caitlin, licking her ice cream.

"Yeah, right," said Brooke with a snort.

"What?" said Caitlin.

Olivia parted the branches of a leafy bush. "He's massaging her shoulders."

"Yeah," said Brooke, "and she looks like she's enjoying it."

Caitlin peered through the bushes. "So?" she said. "There's no law against it."

CHAPTER TWENTY-EIGHT

A skittish breeze puckered the surface of the water and rippled through the willows along the riverbank. A pair of paradise ducks pecked at the grass, honking to one another and a golden retriever, tongue lolling, loped ahead of a boy cycling along the grassy track beside the river.

Caitlin and Liam stepped aside to let the boy pass, then stopped to get their bearings.

"Tolley Drive starts about here," said Liam, pointing through the trees. "Connor Sampson's house is about halfway down, opposite the reserve."

"Right," said Caitlin, marching on.

Liam hesitated. "What if he's home?"

Caitlin frowned. "C'mon, don't chicken out now."

"I'm not. I came here the other day didn't I?"

"Yeah, well if he's there, we can just wait around till he goes out."

Liam sighed. "Right."

Moments later they were standing across the road from a low brick house, with a tiled roof and double garage. Like all the others in the wide, leafy street, it looked new, spacious and very secure. The garage door was open and a late- model silver SUV was parked on one side and a smaller saloon on the other. No sign of any bikes as far as Caitlin could see.

"Looks like someone's home," said Caitlin.

"Right," said Liam. "Let's wait in there." He pointed to the entrance to a reserve.

They headed down a path that led to a flat grassy area fringed by rockeries of native flaxes and grasses of yellow, green and a pretty deep copper. Near the entrance was a children's playground, its barked surface covered in brightly coloured plastic play equipment. Caitlin noticed that, unlike most of the parks she was used to, there wasn't a scrawl of graffiti in sight.

Liam set down the backpack and lowered himself onto a swing. Caitlin folded her arms and sat on a platform below an abacas of giant coloured beads.

She suddenly had an attack of the nerves. "What if he's not the guy?" she said, beginning to gnaw a ragged fingernail.

"He's the guy," said Liam, closing his eyes as the swing arced slowly. "Why else would he have those bikes?"

"I didn't see any in the garage."

"They're down the back, in the corner."

"Right." Caitlin abandoned her fingernail and picked up a twig. She began probing a hole in the timber, disturbing a column of ants, which began scurrying frantically and waving their legs in protest.

Half an hour later, Liam was sitting on the top of the slide and Caitlin was dozing in the sun when they heard voices. Caitlin leapt up and shielded her eyes from the sun.

"They're going out," she called to Liam.

Trying not to be too obvious, he edged around a bush and peered across the road. They saw a dark, thickset man climbing into the SUV and a much younger, red-haired woman helping two small children into the back.

Caitlin swallowed. "Right, let's go," she said, grabbing the backpack.

As they got closer to the house, Caitlin stopped and ushered Liam forward. "Come on," she said, "you know the way."

Glancing around quickly to check that they weren't being watched, Liam led the way down the side of the house, through a spring-loaded iron gate and into a tidy, secluded yard. There was a large paved area close to the house. 'Ideal for outdoor entertaining,' a real estate brochure might have crowed. In the middle was a big round metal and glass table and six chairs with puffy green-and-white striped cushions. Near the sliding door was a barbecue with a domed metal hood. Beyond, a circular trampoline sat on the well-kept lawn, alongside a metal swing set and a child's ride-on car, lying on its side.

One wall of the garage bordered the yard and in the middle was a window, through which Liam was already peering. "Here, look," he said, shielding his eyes from the sun. Caitlin, her heart hammering, slipped in beside him and peered into the dark interior. It took a while for her eyes to adjust and take in the jumble of contents. There was garden equipment, tins of paint, a boogie board, a broken highchair, two foam mattresses wrapped in plastic, some rolls of carpet, an old gas heater, stacks of cardboard boxes and a new-looking electronic exercise bike.

"Over there," whispered Liam, pointing to the left back corner. There, stacked neatly against the wall, Caitlin could see a dozen or more bicycles, their seats wrapped in plastic and with sales tags hanging from their handlebars. She didn't need to see the brand name to recognize what they were.

In spite of her ragged nerves, she felt a sudden thrill. She steadied herself against the wall and turned to Liam. "They're Trailblitzas all right. Let's get some shots of them."

"Bit dark," said Liam, "but I'll give it a go." He lifted his camera to frame a shot, when he was interrupted by someone clearing his throat. Caitlin and Liam spun around to see two policemen, their arms folded and eyebrows raised in silent enquiry.

As they were led to the police car, Caitlin saw a

shadow move behind a curtain of the house next door.

~

CAITLIN SAT cross-legged on her bed recovering from the big row downstairs. Her mum had gone ballistic when she arrived home in a police car. She accused Caitlin of being totally irresponsible and of causing extra stress, which she sure as hell could do without.

Surprisingly, Granddad had stuck up for Caitlin. "If you people had done the job you're paid to do," he'd said to the two policemen who dropped her home, "it wouldn't have been left to a thirteen-year-old to go looking for answers."

After they'd gone though, he changed his tune and told Caitlin she'd been thoughtless and he expected better. The conversation ended when the phone rang and Caitlin took the opportunity to slip out of the kitchen. She grabbed a tissue and blew her nose.

Her phone beeped a text. It was Liam.

U still alive?

Caitlin managed a smile and replied: *Just.*

My olds flipped said Liam.

Same

Wot did ur mum say?

Went ballistic. I'm grounded.

Me 2 & Play Stn band

Ouch

I told them it was all yr idea

Funny, replied Caitlin, *I told Mum it was yrs.*

She heard a car in the driveway.

GTG, she texted.

She pulled back the curtain and looked down on the driveway. Phil was getting out of his vehicle. She flicked off the intercom, eased her legs under the covers and closed her eyes.

Some time later she woke with a start when her bedroom door opened. It was Phil. He smiled sympathetically. "Hiya, troublemaker."

Caitlin hoisted herself into a sitting position and hugged her knees. Her eyes felt sticky, her lips dry and she was still groggy with sleep.

"Oh dear," said Phil. "Don't think a life of crime suits you."

Caitlin gave him a fierce look and lowered her head onto her knees.

"Dinner's ready," he said. "You coming down?"

"Not hungry," said Caitlin, sullenly. Her stomach rumbled in dissent.

"It's shepherd's pie," he said, looking from under his brows. Caitlin didn't answer. "And cheesecake."

Caitlin's stomach pleaded with her but she ignored it and continued to scowl, refusing to meet Phil's eyes.

"Damn," he said, pursing his lips. "I was sure the cheesecake would work."

Caitlin slid down and pulled the duvet over her head.

"Right," said Phil. He headed for the door then stopped. "So this means I can have your cheesecake?" He shut the door quickly as a woolly slipper thudded against it.

~

HUNGER FINALLY DROVE CAITLIN DOWNSTAIRS. It was late. Phil was loading the dishwasher and Granddad had gone to bed. Her mother, who was working on the computer, looked up as Caitlin came into the room. She didn't look happy.

"Your dinner's in the microwave," she said, "although Skoota almost got it."

"He would've had to fight me off," said Phil. Nobody laughed. He cleared his throat and concentrated on squeezing the last mug into the rack.

Caitlin scoffed down her dinner then began exploring the fridge to see if there was any cheesecake left. Phil looked guilty and began whistling. Caitlin flashed him a resentful look and then began digging in the freezer for some ice cream

"You can forget that," said her mother sternly. "I need to talk to you."

"Right, I'm going to head off," said Phil, giving the bench a final dramatic sweep with a dishcloth. He gave her mother a quick, companionable kiss, grimaced at Caitlin and hurried out the door.

"So, what were you doing there?" Caitlin's mum asked for the third time. They'd adjourned to the lounge for the interrogation. Caitlin, arms folded, continued to stare straight ahead.

Her mother changed tack. "Look, I know you've been upset about what happened and all that, but you can't just take the law into your own hands and go snooping around people's houses."

"He's not just anyone," said Caitlin angrily. "He sells dodgy bikes."

"You don't know that."

"I do. He's got heaps at his place."

"Look, maybe – just maybe – there was something wrong with that bike – my bike – but it's a huge leap to say 'he sells dodgy bikes'."

Caitlin took a deep breath. "Peter Lee's was a Trailblitza as well."

"Who?"

"Peter Lee, the famous jazz pianist."

"What are you talking about?"

"He crashed and broke both his arms."

"But you don't know—"

"Mum, the handlebars broke off."

"Really?"

"Yes. In the same place as yours."

"How do you know all this?"

"I met him."

"When? Where?"

"Me and Megan did. And someone else complained to that TV show about a Trailblitza."

Rita ran her fingers through her hair. Just then the phone rang. Caitlin stomped into the hall and picked it up.

"Sorry to ring so late," said a male voice, "it's Constable Kane here." Caitlin swallowed. "I'm after Caitlin Nove."

Caitlin's stomach did a flip. She glanced into the lounge where her mother was reading. "That's me."

"Good. Now Caitlin, I believe you were in a bit of trouble today?"

"Yes," muttered Caitlin, feeling suddenly hot.

"I've just come on duty and have been reading the report."

"Mmmm."

"It says your reason for being at Sampson's house was because you were doing some investigation into faulty bikes. Is that right?"

"Yes."

"Well, I think I have to take some of the blame for that."

"Eh?"

"I don't know if you remember me but I came to your house to bring the bike back after we investigated your mother's accident?"

Caitlin recalled the young, dark-haired constable being given a hard time by Granddad. "Yes," she said, "I remember."

"Right, well I also remember suggesting you check out that bike – and why the handlebars broke off."

"Just a minute," said Caitlin, lowering the phone and putting her hand over the receiver. Her mother was beside her, demanding to know who she was talking to. "It's the police," she hissed impatiently.

"Great," said her mother, rolling her eyes and slowly pushing herself back into the kitchen.

"Sorry," Caitlin said into the receiver.

The policeman wanted to know what Caitlin had found out. So she told him about Peter Lee and the complaint to the TV show and how she'd gone to the Ministry of Consumer Affairs. She also told him about how her granddad had dumped the bike and there wasn't any evidence.

There was a short silence as the policeman seemed to be scribbling down some notes. "Right," he said. "Now look, I think I can help. I took a whole lot of photos of your mother's bike, close-ups of the weld that broke, serial numbers and everything. I'm happy to give them to you as long as you promise you'll go about this investigation through the proper channels."

"I will," said Caitlin, earnestly.

"It's important, Caitlin. You can't go trespassing on private property."

"Yes, I mean, no."

"Okay . . . well, I'll put these in the post."

"Cool," said Caitlin. "Thank you."

CHAPTER TWENTY-NINE

Caitlin opened the door to find Megan standing there. She was in her work clothes: a black skirt, high-heeled pointy boots and a long black coat. Her hair was pulled up into a loose topknot and a few loose strands cascaded in flame-coloured corkscrews down her face. "Are you sure this is okay?" she asked, stepping inside. "I thought I wasn't very popular around here."

"It's cool," said Caitlin. "Granddad's gone home and Mum's having a driving lesson in her new car."

"Car?"

"Yeah, you know, with hand controls."

"Cool. Is she getting some help with buying it?"

"Yeah. Phil's . . ."

"No. I mean, you know . . ." Megan rubbed her thumb and fingers in a money-sorting gesture.

"Oh yeah. I think some government place is giving her a grant or something."

"Good," said Megan. "That's good."

Caitlin hadn't seen Megan for a few weeks. Since the incident with the police, Mum and Granddad had been keeping very close tabs on her. There were all sorts of new rules about coming home straight after school and every time she took a phone call, one of them seemed to be hovering in the background. Megan was right to think she wasn't very popular. Caitlin's mum had told her that her friendship with the young journalist was 'inappropriate'.

Megan slipped off her coat and looked around for somewhere to hang it.

"Just dump it on the chair there," said Caitlin. "Do you want a coffee or something?"

"That would be great," said Megan, rubbing her hands together

Caitlin turned on the gas heater in the lounge and left Megan flicking through the police photos as she went to make the coffee. As she was setting out the cups Megan came in to the kitchen, a huge grin on her face. "These are brilliant," she said. "Who says crime doesn't pay?"

Caitlin grimaced. "Granddad, for one – and Mum."

"Were they really upset?"

"'Extremely disappointed'," said Caitlin, mimicking a stern voice.

Megan laughed. "Well, it was pretty brave, what you did. What's happened to Liam?"

"Grounded big time."

"Oh dear," said Megan, accepting a cup of steaming coffee. "I remember being grounded once. For setting fire to the curtains."

"True?" said Caitlin offering sugar.

Megan spooned two heaped teaspoonfuls into her cup. "Yeah, the Fire Brigade came and everything."

"Holy-moley."

"I was only trying to melt a candle to wax my legs."

Caitlin laughed. "Sounds pretty hairy."

Megan groaned. "Yeah, good one."

Back in the lounge, Megan and Caitlin looked more closely at the police photos. They focused on several close-ups of the weld that had held the handlebars on. One picture showed where the weld had just sheared through, leaving a jagged scar of dull grey metal.

"You know, that break is in exactly the same place as the handlebars Peter Lee showed us," said Megan. She squinted closely at the photograph. "Definitely something wrong with that weld."

"Exactly," said Caitlin. "And didn't that TV guy reckon it was the same with the bike he heard about?"

"Yeah," said Megan. "He couldn't remember much but he said it was definitely something to do with the handlebars. Right," she said, tucking a stray ringlet behind her ear. "I reckon we've got enough to go public."

"Public?" said Caitlin.

"Yeah."

"You mean in the paper?"

"Uh. Yeah."

"Shouldn't we go to Consumer Affairs first?"

"Why?" asked Megan. "Were they particularly interested when you phoned them?"

"Well, no," said Caitlin. "Not really." She remembered the patronizing tone of the woman on the phone and how she had been fobbed off.

"So," said Megan, "that's settled."

"But—"

"What?" asked Megan.

"I promised the police I'd go through the proper channels."

"These are the proper channels," said Megan, slurping her last mouthful of coffee and setting the mug on the bench. "You'll see."

In the small, glass-walled office off the news room, Megan sat across the desk from the editor, Marcel Rogan. He was a slight man with sharp features, intelligent eyes, and a neatly trimmed grey beard, which he had a habit of stroking as he spoke.

Megan had told him of her suspicions about the Trailblitzas, about Rita Nove's and Peter Lee's accidents and about Caitlin's role in the investigation. He'd listened intently but now he had his head cocked on one side, pursing his lips and stroking his beard.

"Two accidents, similar circumstances. Could be just coincidence," he said. Megan moved to the edge of her chair and leaned forward. "I've seen both bikes and the break in the weld is identical. Karl reckons he came across another one when he was working for Scam Busters."

"Is anybody investigating?" asked Marcel. "Police? Consumer Affairs?"

"No," said Megan. "Not yet, although the police clearly have suspicions about the bike. They tipped Caitlin off in the first place."

The editor picked up a hacky sack and tossed it from one hand to the other. "It's risky," he said. "If we're wrong, the manufacturer or the seller – or both – could sue."

"We're not wrong," said Megan. "Trust me."

Marcel Rogan smiled wearily and looked across the desk at the young woman with wild hair sitting before him. He'd chosen Megan from over a hundred applicants for a junior reporter's job five years ago and he'd never had a moment's regret. She'd fast gained a reputation as a hard worker with a nose for a good story. He flung the hacky sack into the air and deftly caught it with a well-practised hand.

"Right," he said. "Let's go with the basic story but for goodness sake just stick to the facts. We'll see what reaction it gets."

Cool," said Megan, leaning forward. "There's just one other thing."

Marcel couldn't help smiling at the earnest young face on the other side of his desk. He sighed, and clasped his hands in front of him. "Yes, Megan," he sighed. "What is it?"

CHAPTER THIRTY

Caitlin stood with her camera pointed down the driveway. Granddad was at the end peering down the road. "I think this is them," he called. He craned his neck, listening intently for the sound of a car.

Caitlin began to jiggle. "Is it, Granddad? Is it?"

"Hold on. Hold on. Yes . . . yes it is."

Caitlin steadied the camera and framed the entrance to the driveway. Seconds later, a stylish, apple-green bonnet nosed into shot. "Cool colour," Caitlin breathed as she pressed the shutter and lined up another shot. As the car edged up the driveway, Caitlin zoomed in to her mum's face behind the wheel. "Smile, Mum!"

Rita Nove bared her teeth in a nervous smile as she brought the car to a rather sudden stop alongside Caitlin. Phil got out and staggered around in a drunken circle, then grasped the veranda post.

"Bit hairy, was it?" asked Granddad, strolling over.

"Once she gets the push and pull functions around the right way, she'll be right," he said.

The window slid down. "Is he being rude about my driving?"

"Of course not," said Phil, winking at Caitlin.

"He is," said Caitlin, "but just ignore him."

She opened the passenger door and slid in beside her mother. "Way cool, Mum," she said, glancing around.

Caitlin's mum proudly showed off the intricacies of her new car. Most importantly, the cup holders, the CD player and the sunroof that slid back at the press of a button. Apart from being new and rather fabulous, the car was just like any other except that it had a lever near the steering wheel, which controlled the foot pedals.

"So this is what you drive with?" asked Caitlin.

"Yes," said her mum, grasping the lever. "You push it down for the accelerator. . ." The car, which was still running, gave a throaty rev. "And push it forward for the brake."

"Cool," said Caitlin. "Can I try?"

"Sure."

Caitlin leaned across and had several goes at operating the lever. With each downward push, the engine burst into life.

"Do you think I'll be able to learn to use hand controls?" asked Caitlin.

"No need," said Mum. "You can use the foot controls. It's dual purpose."

"Mint," said Caitlin beaming, "and I so love the colour."

"Isn't it fabulous?" enthused Mum. "Couldn't decide between this and the magenta but think I made the right choice."

There was a burst of laughter outside. It seems the men found the conversation drifting out of the sunroof amusing. Phil opened the door. "Glad you like the colour, girls, but we're more interested in what's under the bonnet."

Caitlin and her mum left Phil and Granddad with their heads under the bonnet while they went inside. As Rita was making the coffee the phone rang. She picked it up and frowned. "Yes, just a moment." She handed the phone to Caitlin. "It's Megan."

Caitlin took the phone, made a face at her mother, and went to sit on the stairs.

"It's all go," said Megan, breathlessly. "The story's scheduled for Saturday."

"Cool," said Caitlin. "What are you going to say?"

"You mean, what are we going to say?"

"Huh?"

"I'd like you to help me write it."

"Me! Why?"

"It's your story. You've done all the hard work. Thing is, we have to stick to the facts. What we can prove . . ."

"Right," said Caitlin.

"But there's one small problem," said Megan.

"Mmm?"

"If you're going to help write this, we need to find another name for you."

"Huh?"

"My editor says we can't use your real name because you're too young. Press Council rules, apparently."

"Oh, right."

"You'll have to use a pseudonym."

"A what?"

"A fake name. You know. Like famous writers who have pen names."

"Cool," said Caitlin.

"So, who do you want to be?"

"Um . . ." Caitlin's mind was a blank. She rubbed the back of her spiky hair and shifted from one foot to the other. "Can I think about it?"

"Sure," said Megan. "But there's not a lot of time. Just let me know when you've decided."

"I will," said Caitlin.

~

Later, when she should have been doing her maths homework, Caitlin sat, pen poised over paper, trying to come up with a suitable name. So far she'd tried Jesse Jarvis, Monique Mystique, Beyonce Barrett and Clarice Carter, but nothing felt right. She liked the intrigue of having a false identity. She imagined a deep movie voice profiling her character: *Caitlin Nove. By day a regular teenager – but behind the mask lurks an intrepid, investigative journalist, busting scams and scandals, catching crooks. Working to make the world a safer place ...*

She snorted and tapped the pen on her teeth. How about Mandy Morris" She wrote it down and studied it for a moment. Nah, sounded like a beautician. She scrunched the paper into a ball and tossed it on the floor to join a scattering of rejects.

Skoota, who was sitting on the windowsill, looked mildly interested for a moment, then yawned and settled his head on his paws.

Caitlin got up and padded into the dining room where her mum was folding a basket of clean laundry that had been sitting on the table for most of the week.

"Here, grab this," she said, holding out a crumpled sheet. Together they folded four sheets then Caitlin stacked them in the linen cupboard.

"What about that lot?" said her mother, gesturing to a pile of Caitlin's gear.

"I'll take it when I go back upstairs," said Caitlin.

"Make sure you do," said her mum. "They've been sitting there all week."

Caitlin rolled her eyes and then headed to the kitchen to make a sandwich. "Want a sammie?" she called to her mother as she smeared butter on the bread.

"No thanks," she answered. "Just get me a yoghurt, will you?"

Caitlin opened the fridge. "Do you want apricot or . . ." She inspected the labels on a four-pack. ". . . apricot?"

"Better give me apricot."

Caitlin broke a pottle from the pack and slid it across the breakfast bar. She opened the cutlery drawer, grabbed a spoon and slid that across as well.

"What did Megan want?" Rita asked, tearing the top off the yoghurt.

"She's doing a story on a terrorist organisation and she wants me to go undercover with her," she said.

"No need to be smart," said her mother. "You know what I think about you associating with her."

"It's cool, Mum. Trust me," said Caitlin, slapping the top on her cheese sandwich. She took it through to the lounge and was about to sink into a worn armchair by the heater when she noticed a newspaper folded on the seat. She picked it up and went to toss it aside when she noticed the crossword, completed in Granddad's tidy writing. She smiled. Down the side as usual, were neat little jottings where he'd worked out the anagrams. "That's it," she muttered to herself.

"What?" called her mother.

"Nothing." Caitlin grabbed a pen and paper from the sideboard and wrote down her name: CAITLIN V. NOVE

She battled for ages with a host of combinations including, NOVA TINVICEL, ANNE VIVLOCIT, VIVIAN CLENOT, but they all sounded like tragic Russian ballet dancers, probably with anorexia and sad love lives.

Caitlin grabbed a clean sheet of paper and wrote her name again.

CAITLIN V NOVE

She folded her arms and studied it carefully. The letters seem to dance in front of her eyes. She blinked, then immediately saw it. Seconds later she was staring at her new identity . . . VIOLA VINCENT . . . and the spooky coincidence that had emerged.

CHAPTER THIRTY-ONE

Saturday morning, Caitlin was up early and almost knocked the delivery boy off his bike as she ambushed him at the gate.

"Oi, watch out," he said, wobbling into the hedge.

"Sorry," called Caitlin, as she jogged back into the house. She wrenched the chunky paper from its wrapping and turned to the inside front page. There was the story. Her story:

Freak Accidents Raise
Questions about Bicycle Safety
Megan Ryan & Viola Vincent Reporting

A young mother is in a wheelchair and the career of a promising pianist hangs in the balance after two freak bicycle accidents within months of one another.

Both victims were riding Chinese-made Trail-blitza mountain bikes and in both accidents the handlebars appeared to shear off under stress.

The first victim, Rita Nove, was riding in Redwood Falls last year when the front wheel of her bike struck a rock on a downhill section of the track and the handlebars broke off. Ms Nove, an occupational therapist, somersaulted over the handlebars and broke her back. She is now confined to a wheelchair.

Internationally acclaimed youth jazz pianist, Peter Lee, was also badly injured when he braked sharply and the handlebars of his bicycle broke off. Mr Lee fractured both wrists and specialists are unsure if he will be able to continue his career.

Richard Carson, President of the Bicycle Importers and Retailers Federation (BIRF), said it was unusual to have two identical bikes fail in the same way. I'll be asking some questions for sure," he told the Courier, "especially when such serious injuries have resulted."

Mr Carson said members of his Federation follow a strict code of practice when importing bikes into the country but he said he couldn't speak for 'rogue importers' who'd been responsible for bringing in substandard bicycles in the past.

Although both incidents have been reported to the Ministry of Consumer Affairs, a spokesman told the Courier that no active investigation is underway. The Ministry says the case may be reviewed if further complaints are received.

The paper had used one of the police photos of her mother's fractured bike. Caitlin was reading the story for about the tenth time when her mother called and she was diverted into the busy morning routine. Later, as she was loading the dishwasher, the phone rang.

"Guess what?" said Megan breathlessly. "We've had calls from three other people with Trailblitzas where the same thing's happened."

"Really?"

"Yeah, listen to these emails."

Caitlin eased herself onto a stool at the breakfast bar.

Megan cleared her throat and began to read: *"I'd like to thank the Courier for exposing the problem with Trailblitzas. I bought one for my 11-year-old son, Sam, last Christmas. About a month later, he had a bad accident when he jumped a ramp at the bike park. The handlebars broke off and he landed on his face, smashing his front teeth. He's had to have extensive (and expensive!) dental work. Until I read your story, I thought Sam must have done something stupid to cause such damage to the bike. His dad and I thought he wasn't telling us the whole truth. Now I realize it was the bike that caused the accident. Thanks so much for exposing this. You've done a huge public service."*

Caitlin couldn't say anything. She was finding it hard to breathe. Tears stung her eyes. She squeezed them shut.

"And this . . ." she heard Megan say: *"I bought a Trailblitza 500 for my daughter, Sophia, 13. After I read your story this morning I went out and checked the bike. The weld, where the handlebars join the frame, is already starting to crack. There's no way Sophia will be riding this bike any more. Thank you so much for bringing this to public attention. I hate to think what might have happened if you hadn't."*

"So there you go," said Megan. "You were right, Caitlin. You were so right." Her voice was thin and shaky.

Caitlin didn't trust herself to speak. All the months of pain and anger swept over her like a spring tide, first engulfing then receding to leave her drained and empty. All she could manage was "Mmm."

"Hey, don't get me started," said Megan. "I'm not wearing waterproof mascara."

Caitlin still couldn't get any words out. "You're a champion," whispered Megan. "We'll talk later, yeah?" and she hung up.

Caitlin sat slumped at the breakfast bar, the phone still in her hand. Her mother was staring at her. "What is it, baby?" she said, wheeling herself around to the other side of the breakfast bar. Caitlin handed her the paper.

By evening the story had made the television news and Megan came around to watch it.

~

Caitlin was relieved to see Granddad greet her warmly as she squeezed between them on the sofa. There was film of a reporter knocking on Connor

Sampson's door and of bikes being removed from his property.

"We'll sue the beggar," said Granddad, waving his fist at the television. Mum winked at Caitlin and Phil smiled and shook his head.

"Well you've done a great job exposing that crook," said Granddad, turning to Megan. "And that Viola Vincent must be quite a reporter," he looked sideways at Caitlin, "and I'll bet she's good at anagrams too."

Megan smiled politely. Caitlin looked coy and concentrated on the screen.

After the news, Megan accepted an invitation to stay for dinner. Granddad reached in his pocket. "My shout. Indian suit everyone?"

"Totally," said Phil, licking his lips in an exaggerated fashion.

Phil went to pick up the meal and Caitlin went with him. As they drove, Phil turned to Caitlin. "You should be very proud of yourself." Caitlin blushed. "Seriously. You've sure got guts, the way you stuck with it."

"I think I'm just stubborn," said Caitlin. "I get it from my dad, apparently."

Phil smiled and changed gear. "Did your Mum tell you about her new job?" he asked.

"No," said Caitlin, eyes wide. "What job?"

"Well," said Phil, smiling, "she really should tell you herself."

"No. What? What?"

"Well, when she tells you, you've got to look surprised, okay?"

"'Course. C'mon."

"She's got a job at the gym."

"The gym?"

"Yeah, as Rehabilitation Coordinator."

"Eh?"

"She designs programmes and looks after people rehabilitating after accidents and stuff."

"Cool."

"It is, eh?"

Caitlin was stoked about her mum's job but, on Phil's instructions, she tried not to look too happy as she skipped up the steps with the takeaways. She needn't have worried – one look at Megan's face wiped any hint of a smile from hers.

"What's wrong?' said Caitlin dumping the curries on the bench.

Megan was clutching her mobile tightly. "The bikes they took from Sampson's," she said. "They weren't Trailblitzas."

"What?" said Caitlin, the colour draining from her face.

"They weren't Trailblitzas," repeated Megan, "and he's threatening to sue."

Caitlin felt like her legs were about to give way. Her brain jammed up. Everybody was looking at her. "But . . . I . . ." she began.

"Why were you so sure they were Trailblitzas, Caitlin?" Megan asked, in a slow deliberate voice.

"Because I saw . . . I think I saw . . ."

"Ohmigod," Megan put her head in her hands.

"It was dark . . . and they were in the corner but . . ."

Megan began to pace. Caitlin started to cry. She was surprised to feel Granddad put his arm around her. He gave her shoulder a little squeeze.

"Caitlin wouldn't get something like that wrong," he said firmly, "and that bloke on the TV tonight is the same bloke I bought the bike from. I'm sure of it."

"You're probably right," said Megan, "but we've got no proof."

Caitlin bit her lip. She tried to picture the bikes in Sampson's garage. She'd been so sure they were Trailblitzas. There'd never been any doubt in her mind – until now.

Suddenly the fog began to clear. She remembered Liam holding his camera up just as the police arrived. "Hold on!" Caitlin yelled and darted out of the room.

Minutes later she watched the photo materialise on the computer screen. She could have hugged Liam. It was dark and badly framed but the word 'Trailblitza' was clearly visible on the frames of the bikes stacked in Sampson's shed. "He must have swapped them," said Megan, "sometime after you'd been there."

"Crafty beggar," said Granddad from behind.

"Thank goodness for this," said Megan, hitting the forward button and sending the photo to her editor. "That was a heart-stopping moment." She hugged Caitlin. "Sorry, I was so . . ."

"It's okay," said Caitlin. "I knew about the photo. I just kind of . . . froze up."

By Monday the Government had ordered a recall of Trailblitza mountain bikes. The story got even more interesting when an American commerce investigator who had seen the story on the Net, contacted the Courier to say that he had been involved with a recall of faulty Trailblitzas in California. "I think the bikes we took off the streets here were shipped to your country and sold," he told Megan. "The importer would have paid next to nothing for them."

Megan and Caitlin wrote a follow-up story that also made the *Courier*'s front page.

American Link to Faulty Chinese Bikes

Megan Ryan & Viola Vincent reporting

A shipment of faulty Chinese bikes, believed to have caused several injury accidents in this country, had already been taken off the streets in the United States.

The Trailblitza 500s were originally sold in California but recalled by commerce investigators after six serious injuries to riders after their handlebars snapped off. The bikes were supposed to have been destroyed but appear to have been resold and shipped to New Zealand.

Federal Investigators have arrested a 43-year-old

U.S. customs official and charged him with theft as a servant and breaches of trade law.

Charges are also pending in this country against Connor Larry Sampson, for breaches of customs and consumer protection laws. Sampson allegedly imported the bikes from the U.S. knowing they were faulty and sold them in a temporary retail outlet last November.

Numerous accidents have been attributed to the faulty bikes, the most serious of which left a young mother paralysed and a promising pianist with fractured wrists.

CHAPTER THIRTY-TWO

"Nice work," said Liam, sidling up to Caitlin in the school tuck shop.

"Shush," said Caitlin. "Don't blow my cover."

"In your dreams," laughed Liam. "Who do you think you are, Jane Bond or something?"

Caitlin giggled. "Thank goodness you took that photo."

"I so nearly deleted it," said Liam. "It was pretty blurry and I have my reputation to think of." He licked his finger and smoothed an eyebrow

"Whatever," laughed Caitlin. You must have clicked just as the cops turned up.

"Just after," he said. Had a feeling we might need some proof.

"You know that nosy neighbour," said Caitlin, "the one who called the cops on us?"

"Yeah."

"She saw Sampson moving the bikes later that evening."

"True?"

"Yeah. She wrote down the exact time, the rego of the van and everything."

"Man," laughed, Liam. "Just the sort of neighbour not to have, if you're into dodgy business."

"I reckon," said Caitlin. "The police tracked the van to a warehouse across town. That's where they found the Trailblitzas."

"So he stacked some other bikes in his garage as decoys?"

"Apparently," shrugged Caitlin, "according to Mrs Spyball from next door."

"Talking about oddball people," said Liam. "Mrs Weavers is looking for you."

"That's mean," said Caitlin.

"But true," said Liam. "See you round."

When Caitlin walked into the library, Mrs Weavers beamed. "That was great work by the Courier cracking the bike story," she said. "That's the sort of journalism you should aspire to."

"Right," said Caitlin, trying to look serious. "They did a good job."

"Now," said Mrs Weavers, hauling a cardboard box full of papers from under her desk, "there's a little issue here that the school council might want to take up . . . diet soda."

Caitlin couldn't remember the last time they'd eaten out at a restaurant, especially one with linen napkins and table service. It'd been Granddad's idea, to celebrate her mum's new job.

Caitlin looked across the table at her mother. Rita was wearing a turquoise top the same colour as her eyes and her hair was scooped into a loose bun. She was grinning at something Phil was saying and their heads were close together. Caitlin still didn't know what was going on between them but she didn't worry anymore. She knew her mum would survive now, whatever happened, and she really hoped Phil would stick around because he was shaping up as a good hockey coach.

He caught her eye and winked. "You okay over there?"

Fine," said Caitlin. "But I'm so starving."

"What's new?" laughed Rita. "What are you having?"

"Lasagne," said Caitlin. "I decided that ages ago."

They were all waiting for Granddad, who was muttering behind a laminated pink menu. "Look at these prices," he was saying. "Absolute robbery."

"Behave yourself, Dad," said Rita. "This is a celebration."

"You're right love. In that case, I'll have the fillet steak."

"Times two," said Phil.

The waitress came and jotted down their order.

"Drinks?" she asked, looking up from her pad. Phil ordered a bottle of wine and Granddad a beer.

"I'll have water," said Caitlin decisively. The waitress left.

"That was a healthy choice," said Mum, looking impressed. "You usually have diet soda."

"Mum," said Caitlin, leaning across the table, "do you know what's in that stuff?"

"Well . . ."

"No, honestly, Mum – you wouldn't be encouraging me to drink it if you knew what was in it." Phil sniggered at Caitlin's indignant face. "It's not funny," she said. "Artificial sweeteners are bad news."

"Right."

"When they're broken down in the body they form neurotoxins that can cause cancer, hyperactivity, irrational behaviour . . ."

"Are you sure you've stopped drinking it?" asked Granddad.

Caitlin flashed him a disdainful glance. "And you know the really scandalous thing?" she continued.

"What?" they all chorused.

"They're going to change all the soda in the school vending machines to diet soda because of the . . ." she hooked her fingers in exaggerated quote marks, ". . . 'obesity epidemic'. How bad is that?"

"Well, good, if it stops kids getting fat," said Phil.

Caitlin rolled her eyes and sighed. "You haven't been listening to a word I've said, have you?" she growled. "They're just swapping sugar for poison!"

Granddad put down his cutlery and smiled with admiration at Caitlin's flushed, earnest face. "I think it's official," he said. "We have another Viola in the family."

– THE END –

THANK YOU!

Thanks for reading *Viola Vincent Reporting*. I hope you enjoyed it!

In book two in the series, *Underdog*, Caitlin, through her alter-ego Viola Vincent, investigates a puppy farm operating in her neighbourhood. She sets out to save Sissy, a young breeding bitch chained to a life of misery.

It is available from all online retailers as an e-book or hard copy.

If you want to know more about me and my writing you can visit my website www.annakenna.com or visit (like and comment!) my Facebook page at www.facebook.com/abkenna54/

Reviews are always welcome—they help me and they help other possible readers to decide if they'd enjoy the book.

Happy reading! – ***Anna***

Printed in Great Britain
by Amazon

73434618R00142